THE WAY OF THE EXPLORER

THE WAY OF THE EXPLORER

THE BEST OF BOTH WORLDS

CHANTAL BARNES

Copyright © Chantal Barnes 2014

First edition 2014
This edition 2015

ISBN 978-1-5147-4533-5

The moral right of the author has been asserted. All rights reserved. This book may not be reproduced in whole or in part without written permission from the author, except by a reviewer who may quote brief passages in a review; nor may any of this book be reproduced, stored in a retrieval system, or transmitted in any form or by any means, electronic, mechanical, photocopying, recording, or other, without written permission from the author.

Editorial: Ilsa Hawtin www.wordsure.co.uk

Cover Design: Helen Nelson www.jetthedog.co.uk

Printed by CreateSpace, an Amazon.com Company
Available on Kindle and online stores

To travel is to live.
    Hans Christian Andersen

Contents

Introduction		1
1.	My Roots	3
2.	A Change of Direction	13
3.	Stuart's Story	19
4.	We Meet Again	23
5.	A Kept Woman	31
6.	The Legendary Glastonbury	39
7.	For Better or for Worse	45
8.	Our Global Honeymoon	51
9.	Mountain-boarding and Mozambique	77
10.	Where to Now?	95
11.	Turkey plucking and Honduras	109
12.	PIG and a Holy Pilgrimage	121
13.	Running for Our Lives	133
14.	A New Direction in Life	175
15.	A Real Life-changer	183
16.	The Earth Moved	195
17.	New Roots	209
18.	No Pressure!	227
19.	So What's It All About?	237

Acknowledgements

Now that I have found the time to write this book to share my life experiences, I especially wish to acknowledge:

Stuart Barnes, my wonderful life partner, who looked after our children while I locked myself away to write these pages. He has provided me with a life that I would never have believed possible, and I am eternally grateful for his love and companionship.

Ilsa Hawtin, who contributed endlessly with her time and editing skills, and kept the flow of the material working all the way through this book.

There are many others who have contributed indirectly with helping me get this book off the press. My parents, Peter and Denise, and my sisters, Weeze, Sasha and Ali, have loved and supported me, no matter what direction my life took. My best friends, Sarah, Amber, Paige, Naomi, Marci, Heather, Adel and Wendy, along with my cousins, especially Margot and Becky, have believed in me every step of the way. My New Zealand family have supported and loved me from the moment we met. My step-daughter, Marie, and her wonderful mother, Kirsten, have always been a big part of our family. And I am blessed to have shared incredible experiences with so many wonderful fellow travellers, all of whom continue to give me inspiration.

Above all, I am grateful to be enriched by my children, who keep me in the moment and fill my life with so much love. They are the true reason this book was created.

Introduction

I was running for my life. If I took a wrong step or turned in a misguided direction, I would be no more – I was sure that the 4,000 lb beast chasing me would pulverise me into a pulp. If someone had foretold this event when I was younger, I would have thought them crazy. But now, as I put every fibre in my being into sprinting faster than I had ever moved, I prayed for some help to get me through this ordeal. Who would have believed that I, a young metropolitan woman of the twentieth century, would be here in the Valley of Heavens, being chased on foot by a wild white rhinoceros?

I had a stable and loving upbringing, then in my mid-twenties my life tilted as I opened up to a new way of living. At the time of publishing this book, I have for 15 years been enjoying six months of travel and six months of work each year ... and currently have no intention of stopping. My journey has taught me many life-enriching lessons, as well as allowing me to discover unbelievable wildlife and cultures all around the world. I've come within feet of wild gorillas in Uganda, hiked some of the highest plains in Ethiopia, and been on a holy pilgrimage to the highest peak of Sri Lanka, to name just a few of the adventures I've experienced.

If you have ever thought about travelling but not known where to start, if you have any misgivings about your work/life balance, or if you sometimes contemplate where your life should be going, you may well take some inspiration from this book. Otherwise, I hope you'll just enjoy reading about the crazy escapades of a girl from Vancouver who chose to explore the world.

Chapter 1
My Roots

Looking back to where it all began, I have to say that I had a very lucky beginning. As is life, we all have the highs and lows that come with growing and learning and figuring out who we are. But to have parents who stayed together as a solid unit, three sisters to play with, and a supportive village of family and friends to surround and guide me, I can see that I was indeed incredibly fortunate. However, in my mind at that time, my childhood was normal.

Growing up, I heard amazing tales from my grandmother, Ruth Rankin about her family and the life they lived. Her grandfather, H.O. Bell-Irving, had been one of the most influential businessmen to emerge from Vancouver, BC, Canada, a city still in its infancy in the late 1800s. He had arrived to help survey the province for the Canadian Pacific Railway in 1885 and, thanks to his entrepreneurial skills, he was able to accrue amazing wealth by canning salmon and selling it throughout the empire. Due to his success, my grandmother experienced a life with governesses, tutors, mansions, balls, exclusive clubs and frequent visits to Europe. What a life! As it happens, most of the money accumulated by my great-great-grandfather had depleted by the time I came into the world, but the best thing he had done was to buy an island off Vancouver, for recreational purposes. Pasley Island is the place that, still to this day, I call home.

My parents brought us up in Vancouver, in a wonderful house adjacent to a park, with distant views of the Pacific Ocean and of the gorgeous mountain backdrop. My father had created his own company and enjoyed working for himself, trading in tools and other hardware products. My mother was a very intelligent high school teacher. My parents' professions allowed us to spend most weekends and the ten weeks of summer on Pasley Island, where we were surrounded by a loving community of family and friends.

Although this may sound luxurious, I need to make a few things clear. There were no vehicles, electricity, televisions or telephones. There were no corner stores or places you could go for entertainment. The children were expected to go outside and play, and not come back until mealtimes. We had to use our imagination to keep ourselves busy from morning to late at night, occupying ourselves outdoors, where we were completely safe from any malicious people or outside dangers. We were on a private island where the only real danger was drowning, so I remember being able to swim almost as soon as I could walk. It was a close community of individuals, where my neighbours were my cousins and their families. The best part for me was that the cousin who lived nearest to me was also my best friend, and she has remained so until this day. It was on Pasley Island that I made all my first experiences of youth, including my first drink of alcohol and my first kiss, and I look back at this time with such fond memories that I wish I could relive them all.

On any weekends we didn't go up to Pasley, I would spend my time together with my family, either at the university pool, where we would challenge each other to jump off the tallest diving platform, or at the Vancouver Aquarium, watching the killer whales or belugas.

After the aquarium we'd sit on one of the many benches and get the squirrels to come to us by knocking nuts together, then squirm as they climbed over our bodies to settle on our heads.

Our grandmother lived just minutes away from our house and was a firm fixture in our lives, joining us for most events and holidays, and spreading her words of wisdom. Her favourite saying was 'You can never be too rich or too thin.' She'd always let the grandkids know when she thought we'd gained too much weight, and she loved to hear about our academic achievements. She was the matriarch of the family and she took her role seriously, sharing her love and giving support to all her kin.

My grandmother's brother, Budge Bell-Irving, was another firm fixture in our lives. He was my dad's favourite uncle, as well as being one of the most popular lieutenant-governors in the history of British Columbia. One of my fondest memories is when he invited all his relatives, including all our aunts, uncles, cousins and our extended family, over to Government House for Christmas. As kids, we thought this mansion was the perfect playground – we would run up and down the hallways, trying not to be caught as we went up and down the service elevator, and scoping out sections of the grounds that were meant to be off limits. Then the music would come on, and we'd all run into the ballroom, spending hours swaying to the tunes, ecstatic to be in each other's company in such extravagant surroundings.

Dancing was a big part of our lives and my parents enjoyed taking us to 'Dinner & Dance' functions. During the Christmas season, we'd all get dressed up in our finest dresses. While these were usually hand-me-downs from our cousins, or dresses bought from charity shops, we felt magnificently attired. We would then attend the 'Family Ball', an evening of fine food and great music, where my father and I were always the first ones on the dance floor. We all loved to dance and we loved music. We harmonised together on car trips or when my mum strummed her guitar or played her piano, and, with our small repertoire of songs that we'd sing at short notice, people often compared us to the Von Trapp family from *The Sound of Music* movie. We would often break out in a tune as we crossed the trails up on Pasley Island, a pastime that distracted us from the length of the journey and from the shadows of the forest.

We were first introduced to music with my dad's 45s – seven-inch records that held voices of artists from the 1950s and 1960s – which we would play on his record player in the living room. Over the years, larger vinyl records came into being, and it was a memorable moment when my dad took my older sister, Anne-Louise (nicknamed 'Weeze'), and me to the Hudson Bay Department store to buy our first records as our birthday presents. My sister chose the latest ABBA record, and I purchased the new *Thriller* album by Michael Jackson. Our music recording progressed in time to audio cassettes, which I'd fill by listening to the radio stations, pressing record at the start of a good song and trying to stop the recording before the DJ started talking. It is amusing, now that iPods and MP3 players have replaced audio cassettes, to remember how cutting-edge they felt just a few decades ago.

After high school, I chose to attend the University of Victoria on Vancouver Island, to continue my education in marine biology and to learn how to fend for myself. One of the biggest turning points at this time in my life came when I decided to travel to Mexico on my own during one of my holiday periods. One of my best friends, Paige, had landed a job at an all-inclusive resort called Club Med, and she was allowed to nominate friends to join her as volunteers. The deal was that, if I could make my own way down to her, I could stay at the resort with free room and board, and enjoy the sunny climes and beaches of the tropical location. My job would then be to look after the children of families visiting the resort, taking them from one activity to the next. It was winter time in Canada, cold and wet, and with three weeks off from university, I decided to join my friend for the holidays.

The first step was the flight from Vancouver to Mexico City. I had never done anything like this on my own before, but started to gain a little confidence as I landed, still in one piece, in this foreign country. I next had to take a taxi to the bus terminal. My newly discovered confidence started to shake a bit as I was driven down the roads of this massive city at over 180 km per hour, as the driver changed lanes randomly without signalling. He blared his horn repeatedly as we narrowly avoided collision after collision. After 45 minutes of a heart-pumping, nail-biting, gripping-my-seat-for-dear life adventure, I was so thankful to be alive and on my feet again, and I thanked the good lord as I entered the massive bus station ready for the next step.

And now came my biggest test. I didn't speak a word of Spanish and trying to locate the right desk to guide me to my final destination, a little town called Zihuatanejo, was proving impossible. After an hour of going in circles, I decided to take a break and go to the bathroom. I was not ready for what awaited me. With nowhere to leave my backpack safely, I had to carry it into the tiny cubicle and try to hover above a tiny hole in the ground where, in my experience, a toilet bowl should have been. The stench was overpowering and I exited the bathroom in stunned disbelief, feeling nauseated and overwhelmed. What on Earth was I doing? I tried for another two hours to find a single soul who spoke English, but luck was not on my side, and I seriously started to doubt my decision to come to Mexico. Nothing was going my way and I remember clearly having to make a momentous decision: either stick it out and follow my friend's footsteps to this remote town, or simply to return to the airport and go back to Vancouver. So here, alone and pretty bewildered in an entirely foreign environment, I made a decision that changed the course of my life. I realised that I just had to believe in myself: if my girlfriend could do it, then I could do it. I went back to the travel desks and persevered until I finally found my bus. Then, after a 12-hour journey, with chickens fluttering down the aisle of the overcrowded bus and with the constant sound of screaming babies, I arrived on the steps of the resort. I had done it.

This experience had a significant impact on my inner confidence. Having grasped the opportunity to start work abroad and overcome the challenging obstacles that nearly made me turn back, I now had gained the confidence to put my hand to anything and everything that life would throw my way, allowing me to believe that I could do anything I set my mind to in the years to come.

During my university years I was able to volunteer at the Club Med resorts in Mexico, the Bahamas, Florida and the West Indies. I had a blast in all these tropical locations, enlisting my sisters and friends to join me on my trips. During the day we'd take care of children and were able to participate ourselves in their activities – everything from trapeze antics to water-skiing. Then we'd stay up late into the night, dancing to the music blasting from the disco, or performing in the nightly entertainment.

I also had time to volunteer at the Marine Mammal Research Group, where I dissected dolphins, porpoises and other marine mammals that had washed up on the beaches, researching the causes of death. I was lucky enough to get a job on a whale-watching boat, where I worked as a naturalist, riding the pontoons of the inflatable zodiac, describing the habits of the killer whales and, with engines turned off, coming within feet of these majestic mammals. I completed my science degree at the University of Victoria with honours, then returned home to work at the Vancouver Aquarium. Again acting as a naturalist, I was responsible for the marine-mammal deck, talking on the microphone to thousands of visitors about the killer whales, pacific white-sided dolphins, belugas and other sea creatures that were in captivity at the aquarium.

At this point I still had no idea what I wanted to do for a career. In the footsteps of my mother, I decided to complete a one-year additional university course to become a high school teacher. I figured that, if I enjoyed it, I would be a biology and maths teacher, and if I didn't like it, then it was only one year out of my life and another degree under my belt. Upon graduation, I began teaching immediately, putting my name on the substitute list in the North, West and Central Vancouver School Districts, and would often get called back to the same schools, filling my calendar to the brim. I enjoyed the challenges of teaching and I loved it when I saw the 'a-ha' moments in my students, but a few years down the road the job became monotonous and I was ready for a new direction in life.

The moment for change came when I received a phone call from one of my best friends, Paige, the same girl I had gone to see in Mexico years earlier. She asked if I could help out her brother, who was managing the Langara Island Lodge, a fishing resort north of the Queen Charlotte Islands in northern British Columbia. They needed someone to go to the lodge for a ten-day period, to help prepare the accommodation and serve the guests, taking on the role of cleaner, hostess, waitress and dish-washer, all wrapped up into one worker. My first reaction was to decline, imagining a stinking, dirty fishing lodge, but I accepted the position as a favour to my friend and to gain a new experience.

My view of the world changed as we flew to the remote lodge on the private helicopter and I spotted humpbacks breaching in the ocean and bald eagles flying past the dark-green treetops. Due to the rotational schedule I fell into, I had one day off during those ten days, and I spent my free time fishing. I was taken aback when my 16-foot boat became surrounded by three pods of killer whales: over 60 whales were spy hopping, tail slapping and moving in my direction. I stayed with this clan for over an hour, and it was at this point that my world again shifted paths. I was hooked.

When I returned to Vancouver, my dad asked what I thought of the experience. When I said that I was going back for a full season, he replied 'Damn, I knew you'd say that!' He had had the privilege of fishing at a similar resort and knew that, if I went to work there, I would have to give up my teaching profession for the six-month fishing season, from April to the end of September. And that is what I did. My lifestyle changed to a rotation of six months working followed by six months off work, the work allowing me to save sufficient funds to plan my next grand adventure and to see the world.

At this stage, I never imagined this lifestyle could go beyond a few years – although I enjoyed working at the lodge, it wasn't a career for life. My fate would have its own destiny, and my life would change gears as my travel adventures ultimately changed my life forever.

Chapter 2
A Change of Direction

A plan came together. I was to go on a six-month adventure with my youngest sister, Ali, and my cousin, Margot, and our task was to see, smell and sense as many new cultures as we could in that time. We put our heads together and soon our destinations were clear: we were heading to Southeast Asia and Australia.

Our first port of call was Bangkok, Thailand, and after staying for a few days with a family friend, we ventured out on our own. Our direction was south, to the Islands of Koh Samui and Koh Phangan, where beautiful beaches and warm seas welcomed us and where my sister and cousin would get certified in scuba diving, joining me in the ranks of a certified Open Water Diver. And it was here that we discovered the real meaning of a Full Moon party. This all-night beach party, taking place once a month on the night of the full moon, was the talk of the backpacker scene.

We counted the days until we could join thousands of other gringos, with DJs coming in from all over the world to play their favourites in psychedelic trance, drum and bass, house, R&B, dance and reggae. As we danced all night long to the epic tunes blasting from numerous bars along the seaside, we rejoiced in our newfound freedom and decided to continue our adventures in the north of the country. Taking midnight buses and trains became second nature to us, and we enjoyed elephant treks and magical lantern festivals as we travelled through Chang Mai and Chang Rai, searching along our route for foreign novelties and delights.

Ali, Margot and I believed we were on a mission, to learn, grow and enlighten ourselves as much as we could while in this country of exotic and foreign culture. I had brought a number of books with me, most of them spiritual works, and we read them out loud together and conversed on the meanings of the books and how they applied to our lives. The books ranged from *The Four Agreements* by Don Miguel Ruiz, *The Seat of Your Soul* by Gary Zukav and *Conversations with God* by Neale Donald Walsch, to *The Way of The Peaceful Warrior* by Dan Millman and *You Can Heal Your Life* by Louise Hay. As we progressed through the chapters, we put some of the ideologies into practice and could see such clear results, watching how others reacted to our words and actions that were so full of intent. We were astounded and humbled by our own powers and could see clearly how we were creating the experiences of our lives.

We returned to Koh Phangan in time for another Full Moon party. It was here that I fell for a younger backpacker, a wonderful individual who put me on a pedestal for being in tune with myself, and who loved being in my company. Ross and I planned our next few weeks together and explored Thailand, Indonesia and the north-east coast of Australia, before committing to each other but going our separate ways. Ross was off to New Zealand, where he had planned an expedition in whitewater-river rafting – his profession and passion. Meanwhile, Ali, Margot and I continued down the east coast of Australia, covering over 3000 km, then hightailed it back to Asia before we used up all our travel funds.

A Change of Direction

We rejoiced in our return to our beloved Bangkok, once again comfortable in our fisherman pants and flip flops, and familiar with our surroundings. We already knew where to eat and sleep and, seeing the hundreds of fellow backpackers on Koh San Road, we felt excited and confident on our path. We decided that our next mission needed to be exploration and, with our *Lonely Planet* guidebook in hand, we focused on Thailand's neighbouring countries: our next destinations would be Laos, Vietnam and Cambodia.

In the north of Thailand we took a speedboat along the Mekong River to Laos, a day's travel that cut through beautiful terrain. We sat on the roof of the speeding vessel, arms wrapped around our knees and with giant smiles on our faces, watching as the river cut passed rugged mountains and green jungles, with the odd village at the water's edge. Laos was a jewel, with amazing scenery and a laid-back atmosphere, and it was the cheapest country we'd yet visited. A stay that was supposed to last three or four nights became nearly three weeks, as we soaked up the relaxed feel and grounded ourselves in our books and our in-depth conversations.

From Laos we made the journey east to Vietnam. Our first port of call was the small town of Hoi An, where Margot became our personal designer: she drew up amazing styles of clothes, which we then had tailored by local dressmakers and placed into our newly purchased suitcases. We must have been a sight – three Caucasian girls with backpacks, all lugging large suitcases behind us – but we didn't care. We loved our new wardrobes of silks and cashmere, and believed we had made the deal of the century in our negotiations with the shopkeepers and tailors. From this small town, we carried on south to the coastal town of Nha Trang, where I was stunned by the beauty of our surroundings, and by the thought that this country had been embroiled in war in its not-too-distant history. As soon as we had dumped our loaded bags in our guesthouse, we walked to the beach and sat down for the first time in the Vietnam sands, falling in love with the views of the islands and the feel of the sea breeze.

And this is where I saw him. A man walked by, wearing a sarong for a skirt and a green hippie hat, carrying an Australian didgeridoo over his shoulders, and I was struck by the feeling that I knew him. In my rational mind, I knew we'd never met, but my intuition was telling me something different and made me focus on him intently. I wasn't looking for a boyfriend – I already had Ross to go back to – but something about this stranger had me transfixed. Slowly, I forced myself to refocus on what my sister and cousin were saying and to forget the stranger.

Fate would play its hand. The following day we boarded the famous *Mama Hans* boat, a full-day booze and pot-smoking tour that transported us to four of the nearby islands and included the most extraordinary seafood smorgasbord we had ever experienced. From the moment we boarded the vessel, I became aware of the presence of the man I had seen the day before and kept watch from the corner of my eye, trying to make sense of the connection I felt towards him. He was with a large group of individuals, males and females, and we laughed as we watched the boys jump off the boat and tackle and play tricks on each other, coming to rest on one of the many life preservers that were thrown out onto the sea. Margot became friendly with one of the other men in the group, and by lunchtime we were a part of their crowd. Looking back, this must have been when the real connection began.

My first conversation with New Zealander Stuart Barnes lasted for several hours and focused on the incredible wonders of life and how we were responsible for creating our realities. I told Stuart that I was in love with a great guy, that I had amazing friends and family, and that I was conscious of being connected to a greater energy. Stuart told me about how he was an independent explorer, with a wonderful family back home who supported him on his adventures. His dream was to go to Africa and work with animals, with his main focus on the wild dogs of Africa. With heads close together, we poured out our individual stories and sat happy in each other's company, sharing a wonderful, no-strings-attached connection.

We were having so much fun partying with this group of fellow travellers that we remained in the coastal town of Nha Trang for a week, deepening our friendships before parting to travel in opposite directions. Ali, Margot and I were heading south to Cambodia, to discover the famous Angkor Wat temple; they were on their way north and then inland to see Laos. We made plans to catch up and go to the final Full Moon party on Koh Phangan and, with a final hug, we parted.

At this time of travel, there were no internet cafés for writing emails or for calls via Skype – postcards or expensive international phone calls were the only forms of communication available. We were used to setting aside one day every month, buying a stack of postcards depicting the amazing sights and creatures of the land, and writing down our tales of adventure to send to our family and friends back home. It was just about impossible to keep in any sort of contact with anyone away from home, and we would just pray that everyone was keeping happy and healthy.

So, three weeks after we had left Nha Trang, on a beautiful day in March, I was happily surprised to see Stuart approaching – a warm smile on his face and his hippie hat firmly in place – as I walked up the beach towards my hut at Great Bay Bungalows, Koh Phangan. He had come! Many days and miles had separated us, but the conversation flowed just as easily as it had when we were last together, and we soon felt completely relaxed in each other's company. The stories of his past and of some of his many adventures became my entertainment for the following days.

I was aware that I had changed during my time in Asia and Australia. I had allowed myself to let go of the more conservative side of my nature, enjoying so many carefree days with fellow 'free spirits', often having in-depth discussions on the meaning of life and how to be more spiritually conscious. The books I had shared with my sister and cousin had opened up a new understanding of the energy that surrounds us and how we could channel that energy in so many positive ways. I now felt an entirely new connection with the world around me; I knew that I held an incredible power, one that would enable me to create my own reality, and I now focused on all the positive energy that surrounded me.

Life isn't about finding yourself. Life is about creating yourself.
George Bernard Shaw

Chapter 3
Stuart's Story

Stuart's upbringing was a novelty to me.

I had grown up in a big city, surrounded by a metropolitan culture. I had enjoyed my high school life, where I excelled in the all-girls environment, being head of class in my lower years, sports captain, and finally ending my senior year as the 'head girl' of the school council. I had lived in the same house from birth until university, and had a full community of close family and friends.

Stuart's upbringing was on the other side of the world and was as different from my own as night is to day. When Stuart was six months old, his sister was four and his brothers were seven and eight, his 64-year-old father took over raising his four children on his own. His father was a war veteran and had spent over 20 years in the army, some of that time as a 'desert rat'. In search of new work, he moved to different locations around New Zealand, instilling in his kids the morals of the importance of looking after family, and giving each of them freedom to stand on their own two feet. Stuart unfortunately had some bad experiences during his school years due to the lack of understanding of dyslexia, from which he suffers, as well as having to cope with bullying. On the whole, his recollections of his time at school are more negative than positive.

At 15 Stuart left mainstream education and his home to become a shepherd, and worked on Clarence Reserve, a 132,000-acre station

The Way of the Explorer

comprising rough mountains and treacherous terrain. He had 16 sheepdogs and four horses of his own, and lived in the rugged bush-style huts there, working with some crazy hillbillies. His duties included capturing wild horses and breaking them in, mustering in the cows and the wild bulls, as well as looking after thousands of sheep. It was here, during his months in the remote outback, that he gained incredible insight into pack animals, watching how his dogs and horses communicated with each other. Since the only connection I had ever had with this type of lifestyle was what I had seen on television, as Stuart told me of his previous life I immediately imagined the film *The Man from Snowy River*. I could envisage Stuart as the lead character, riding his horse down a sharp incline, perfectly at ease despite the challenging conditions, with stock-whip in hand and cowboy hat firmly in place.

Soon after his father passed away, Stuart decided to flip a coin to see where life was going to take him: heads, he would use the hard-earned money he had saved to buy himself a new truck; tails, he would go and travel. He flipped the coin a number of times until he got the desired result and, at the age of 18, packed his backpack, waved goodbye to his family and left New Zealand. Stuart's first stop was Alberta, Canada, where he would work on a ranch and develop his lifestyle: six months' work followed by six months' travel … a pattern that has continued throughout the decades until the present day.

Stuart's periods of travel have taken him to many wondrous places, from the Inca trails of Peru to the golden palaces of the Russian Czars and the underground cities of Turkey. But the one continent that continues to this day to draw at his soul is Africa. At the age of 23 he hitchhiked from Egypt to South Africa, an incredible journey through 11 countries. This trip involved amazing as well as frightening times, as he travelled on his own through two war zones, including Rwanda in 1995, a setting of horrifying genocide. But he describes this journey, above all else, as the one that changed his life. It was the one that taught him to enjoy every moment of life and that we should be grateful for everything that we have and receive. One of the other things it gave him was confidence that he could do anything he put his mind to. Since then he has continued to travel all over the world, seeing and experiencing close to 100 countries.

When our paths first crossed, in 2000, Stuart had just come from India and Nepal, a trip of incredible juxtaposition: he had had a meeting with the spiritual leader, the Dalai Lama, and he had witnessed explosive rockets fly overhead in the war-torn municipality of Srinagar.

These life stories unravelled as we sat beside each other, fruit smoothies in hand, on the beaches of Vietnam and Thailand, and I became more and more convinced that this man was something special.

Chapter 4
We Meet Again

Returning to work at Langara Island Fishing Lodge in northern British Columbia, after six months of travel in exotic hot climes, was a challenge. Gone were the days of lying in hammocks for hours, thinking we were solving the world's problems in our heated discussions, only to change gear and order a delicious meal at one of the many seaside restaurants. Gone, too, were my endless nights with friends on the beach, fire-dancing on the cool sands while we watched the twinkling stars reflected in the blue seas. My life had changed drastically and, in the cold, remote northern island landscape of British Columbia, it took only a few weeks before the six-day work week, with 12–14-hour work days, took over my psyche. I started to forget the amazing adventures and new global connections I had made, as I focused instead on the day-to-day struggle of making it through my gruelling work shifts. When I did have a few hours to spare between my shifts, I would return to my new activity of practising with my *poi*, moving the tethered weights around my body until I felt confident enough to do it with fire. Spinning fire was my new passion. I loved it when the fire moved around me, following my movements, its roaring hiss spinning on either side of me, until the fuel was used up and the *poi* burnt out.

As weeks rolled into months, new friendships and new plans for travel developed as a close new friend, Amber, joined me in planning another global adventure. Amber was a kindred spirit, a wonderful, bright soul who loved to travel, party and spread positivity. We had fun naming all the places in the world we dreamed of visiting one day, and then researching potential employers. We sent out cover letters and resumes and, upon the acceptance of our employment by a lodge in the Marlborough Sounds of the South Island of New Zealand, we began to make a plan: we would spend a month in Thailand before heading to New Zealand to work for five months. Amber had travelled on her own before but had never experienced Thailand or New Zealand, and I wanted to revisit the beautiful Asian country that I had fallen in love with a year earlier. I also knew that Stuart would be in Thailand in the same month, as he was endeavouring to start up a company, the School of Travel, with the goal of teaching students how to travel without impacting local culture. The backpacker scene had started taking its toll in a number of countries, with the excessive partying, drug abuse and use of local prostitution. I felt it was important to see Stuart again since he had struck a chord within me, a feeling of familiarity that I just couldn't ignore.

I still felt unsure about which path my heart should take, so I kept in touch with both Ross and Stuart while I was working in the remote north of BC. Every two weeks I would make two international calls, one to Oregon in the United States, where Ross was a river-rafting guide, and the other to England, where Stuart had returned to work and replenish his travel funds. I was keeping a connection open with the two men who had crossed my path, trying to figure out which one would make the better match. They were both incredible men, and I would romanticise about my future – my choice of relationship would inevitably make a drastic difference to my lifestyle.

I also had another focus while working in northern BC. My older sister and best friend, Weeze, was getting married in August, and my wedding gift was to supply all the salmon for the 200 guests. Weeze and I had shared accommodation while attending university in Victoria, and had then become roomies again when we returned to Vancouver, bringing her fun-loving and outgoing match, Rob, into our circle. I had lived with Weeze and Rob for three years, loving our closeness and friendship as we entertained countless guests, making the most of being young in a vibrant city. So in my week off work on Langara Island, instead of staying back to look after the Prime Minister of Canada, who had booked into the lodge, I flew to celebrate a wonderful union with my family. I was delighted to be a part of the revelry and I was proud of my catch – the salmon was a big success. I returned to Langara Island and, as the weeks ticked by, my focus was drawn to my upcoming travels.

Ross had travelled to see me for a few days in Vancouver on my return from Asia. Six months later, in the week prior to my departure for the Orient, I travelled down to Oregon to visit Ross and see if what we had found together could keep us united, even though distance and time would stand against us. We had a great week rediscovering one another and I found myself once again being put on a pedestal, a position I'd never had with any boyfriend in the past. As I left Oregon my mind and heart were in turmoil, trying to make sense of the direction my life should take, whether it was enough to be worshipped by this younger man, or whether I needed to be challenged in another way.

Thailand welcomed me back with open arms and, as I changed from my jeans to my fisherman pants, I immediately felt connected once again to this exotic culture and beautiful race of people. Our first adventure took Amber and me north by train to a remote village,

The Way of the Explorer

where Stuart and his partners had already made a connection with the locals and were teaching the young children English in a free camp within their schools. We made incredible relationships with the kids there and, after a week of school activities, we left with tears in our eyes and smiles on our faces. We were bound for the island life and for my fourth Full Moon party.

By this stage we were almost into our third week of our Asian travels, yet Stuart and I had still not reconnected as we had the year before. Questions started to surface in my conscience: was that first trip a real representation of this individual, or had we just been ships passing in the night, enjoying a short dance in the moonlight before moving on to the real world? Stuart must have felt it too; I caught him walking towards the exit of the bungalows, backpack firmly in place, ready to leave on his own without even a goodbye. It was this rash decision on his part that got my back up and, as I stood blocking his path, I felt a twinge of anger. I had travelled across the globe to see him, as well as making the effort of phoning him over the summer – the least he could do was to give me the next 24 hours, the night of the Full Moon party, before he left! He didn't respond immediately but, after a few moments of consideration and with a sharp nod of his head, he turned back to his bungalow.

My younger sister, Ali, had returned with her new boyfriend to join us for the monthly beach party. In our best dancing outfits we all jumped on the back of the truck, our taxi service that would take us across the island, dropping us off beside the blaring speakers and the pounding of the drums. And so we partied. Hour after hour of lively dancing, moving our bodies to the rhythms that were pulsing down the sands, smiling with the freedom and magic of life.

As the sun rose across the sea, bringing shafts of pinks and red across its surface, Stuart finally opened himself to me and accepted me into his life. In a moment of clarity and presence, he reached towards me and thanked me for still being with him. He said it felt as if a veil had lifted from his conscience and that he was thankful that I was still there, dancing in front of him, happy to be alive, happy to be in his presence; that I hadn't turned away from him as he had been prepared to do only a few short hours earlier. His newfound awareness came with the acceptance that life had drastically changed with our meeting and that a new path was being created for the two of us to walk together. The stranger had left to be replaced by the man who was already familiar to me, a man who was inexplicably connected to my soul on a subconscious level. I felt this unique connection in every fibre of my being, a feeling as if I had known him for many lifetimes.

From this point on, Stuart and I were committed to each other. A few days later the two of us escaped to a distant island paradise on the west coast of Thailand, away from my travel companion and my sibling, and spent a week connecting with each other like never before. This was the first time Stu and I had been on our own, with no other fellow travellers, and we were able to learn and share intimate details on a new level, sealing our relationship and making a serious commitment to one another. This was a man who inspired me, who pushed me to seek more out of myself and out of life. My decision was made: this was the one.

Our month in Thailand came to an end and, even though I was sad to leave this beautiful paradise, I was looking forward to our next port of call, New Zealand, known by the native Maori people as the 'island of the long white cloud'. I was excited to learn that Stu would also be returning to his homeland, and that we would make a connection while we were there. Perfect timing.

The raw beauty of New Zealand stunned me. I had been accustomed to spectacular scenery in my home country of Canada and felt that, if I could take all the best parts of Canada, from the majestic mountains, glaciers and river-cut canyons to the white beaches, islands and lakes, and put them all within a short driving distance, it would make New Zealand. The country comprises two long, narrow islands, one above the other, with the northern part of the North Island made up of tropical climes, and the south of the South Island being one of the land masses closest to Antarctica, with the odd iceberg floating by.

When Amber and I arrived at our new place of employment, we were informed that we were not needed for another two weeks, and were shocked by the generosity of the Kiwis. Despite having known us for only 24 hours, they lent us a vehicle, tent, camping gear and all the connections we would need to enjoy our time touring the South Island. What a hospitable country!

After work had begun, Stuart and I reconnected by phone and made plans for me to visit him and his family near Christchurch, the largest city on the South Island. I remember the day when I travelled down the coast by bus, shocked to find Stuart and his brother greeting me with bare feet, my first lesson in New Zealand way of life. I was nervous at first, but his sister and brothers soon made me feel very welcome. The days passed quickly as I was escorted around the countryside, sitting on the back of a quad bike, enjoying the rolling landscape and the new experiences of farm life. It would be my first close-up encounter with sheep and cows, and the small creek introduced me to my first despised nemesis; the sand fly is a terrible little insect that bites your exposed skin and causes you to itch for days. During this time Stuart and I made new plans for the future. Instead of returning to work at the fishing lodge, I would go to England to stay with Stuart in the south-west county of Devon.

I returned to work at the lodge in the remote Marlborough Sounds in New Zealand, but after a few months Amber and I felt that we were missing out on experiencing this beautiful country as we were far from the sights and sounds of the people. Luck was on our side: one of our co-workers, Gina, invited us back to live with her and her parents, Helen and Clarry, in a one-bedroom ship's quarters that was placed in the backyard of their home in Blenheim. There we worked on fruit farms and at one of the many wineries in the region, picking grapes in the sunshine while listening to music on our Walkmans.

The next few months passed quickly as we filled our days with work and new adventures with Gina and her best friend, Sarah, who was an amazing singer and performed at a high-class restaurant every Friday night. We enjoyed our days off at the local watering holes and filled our evenings with live music and dance. It was with a heavy heart that I would say farewell to my newfound family members, my 'adopted New Zealand parents and sister'. But any gloom was short-lived as I joined my Canadian mum and dad for a tour of the North Island, driving them from one scenic location to the next, all of us in awe of the beauty of this country.

Chapter 5
A Kept Woman

'Surprise!' I will never forget the look of disbelief on my older sister's face as I was brought out of my hiding spot, coming to stand in front of her at her 30th birthday party, while the rest of the family looked on with smug smiles as they had helped keep my arrival secret. I had returned to Vancouver for two weeks, during which time it had been my wish for Stuart to meet my family and to see Pasley Island before I returned with him to the UK, so he had made the necessary arrangements and come to Vancouver, meeting my extended family as well as making time to meet with his business partner to plan the next stage of development for their travel company, School of Travel Ltd. Soon after he left, it was time for me to fill my suitcase with everything I would need for my move to the United Kingdom. This was a huge step for me – I had never moved to live in a foreign country for a man, but I rationalised that, if things didn't work out for Stu and me, I would just have to find a new opportunity along the way.

The plane ticket had been bought and my passport held the crucial document to allow me entry into the UK: my two-year working visa. Luck was on my side on this – I was one year over the age limit to get a two-year working visa, but fortunately one of the guests at the lodge was a high-ranking employee of the UK Consulate. Through this contact, I was able it get this vital stamp; otherwise, things might have worked out very differently.

Stuart met me with a bunch of red roses at Heathrow airport, welcoming me to London on a cold and drizzly afternoon. We drove to the south-west of the country, the four-hour car journey speeding by as we caught up with each other's lives since our parting in Canada. As we turned off the M5, the main highway leading into the counties of Devon and Cornwall, the passing landscape grabbed my focus. I was surprised by the rolling hills, the paddocks that flowed from one into the other and, above all, by the lack of trees. In lieu of the deep-green forests of home, where you can feel at one with nature when surrounded by stillness and peace, we were now surrounded by cultivated farmland. It brought into perspective the long history of this area, a complete contrast to my home town of Vancouver, which had been incorporated as a city only within the last 150 years.

As we drove up a steep hill near the Devon coast, the car slowed and then stopped in front of three houses that were attached to one another. My home for the next six months would be one of the upstairs apartments, comprising two main rooms: a living room with a side stove and fridge unit, and a bedroom; the bathroom was shared with the downstairs tenant. Although I found the space small and cosy, I would focus on the outside; the view from the massive window revealed rolling hills that overlooked the majestic Atlantic Ocean, a scene that brought me peace and tranquillity whenever I looked at it.

For the first time in my life, I became a 'kept' woman. I had the time to read and to work on an Open University correspondence course, achieving diplomas in sports massage and sports physiology, as well as making it to the second level in my Seichem/Reiki training. I was given puppies and lambs to look after, and loved my new position as farmer's girlfriend. I welcomed any orphaned animal into my circle, including 'Rasher', a large pot-bellied pig that came running whenever he saw me come outside. Stuart worked as the outside manager for a tourist farm called 'The Big Sheep' and was responsible for the 11 daily shows, such as horse whispering, dog trialling and sheep shearing, as well as being in charge of the animal welfare of the many farm animals on site.

It was here that I came to appreciate his incredible understanding of and connection with animals, especially when I saw him work with a horse that was about to be put down due to its extremely aggressive kicking and biting behaviour. When this large animal was brought into the circular arena it went on the attack, trying to kick Stuart with its front and back legs as well as lunging forward to take a bite out of him. I was a nervous wreck at the beginning, afraid of the massive, aggressive beast, and was amazed by the end of the 30-minute session, watching as the horse submitted to Stuart and then calmly followed him around the ring like a tame pet. A newfound appreciation for Stuart's skills became lodged into my subconscious, giving him the reins to direct me when it came to anything animal-related in the future.

While Stuart was at work, I would plan our next adventure or activity for his days off. We would pack a suitcase and become tourists, discovering the Welsh coastline or visiting the Roman Baths in the city of Bath, in addition to attending the festivals of the land, my first one being the V Festival. Big acts like Coldplay, Crowded House, Faithless, Texas and the Red Hot Chilli Peppers were all brought together in one venue, and the pulse of the crowd was electrifying, giving us the energy to dance for endless hours, young and carefree and loving every minute. Stuart also scheduled some of his days off to visit his daughter, Marie, in Germany, flying over to see her at least three times per season.

We also found the time to travel to Amsterdam. This was a real eye-opener for me – I was astonished by the openness of the Red Light District, seeing women prostitute themselves from behind glass walls, sitting on a stool or posing, waiting for any man to catch their eye and then pay for their 'services'. I was also shocked by the openness of the Amsterdam 'coffee shops'. With drugs being seen in such a negative light worldwide, I couldn't believe it was possible to go to a café and get a menu that was filled not with food or drinks, but with different strains of marijuana, to be ordered and smoked with the pipes provided. Our last trip together within the season was a four-day excursion to Ibiza, Spain, where we enjoyed sangria and relaxed on loungers beside the hotel pool as music floated through the air.

In the last days of summer, we agreed on an unexpected exchange with Stuart's eldest brother, Garry, who was desperate for cash to continue to grow his mountain-boarding project in New Zealand. In return for the funds Stuart sent to Garry, we received six large mountain boards shipped from the other side of the world. With only a few weeks left in the country, Stuart travelled to a number of surfing spots along the coast trying sell these novelty boards. He was disappointed not to find any buyers, and the boards were packed up with all our other things to be stored at a friend's place for the winter season.

It was strange at first to be a foreigner in an English-speaking country, where I would hear so many different dialects. At times I couldn't make out what was being said or even if it was in English! But as time passed, I started to become familiar with the local accents and could contribute to a conversation, rather than simply smiling and nodding.

The days fell quickly into one another and, as the summer months passed by, the focus started to move to planning our next six months off. Stuart had usually travelled on his own, but over the past couple of years had included one or both of his two best friends, Tony and Duncan, on his trips. Tony was a long-haired Australian hippy, whom Stuart had picked up hitchhiking when he travelled around the perimeter of Australia for a year in a Kombi Van. Stuart liked to joke that he hadn't been able to get rid of him since that trip – the longest hitchhiker he'd ever had.

Tony was our neighbour in the downstairs flat in the house in Devon and also worked under Stuart's management at the Big Sheep tourist farm. Duncan was a fellow Kombi owner and traveller, and had connected with Stuart on the same Australian trip. With his shaven head and thick Norfolk accent, and ready for any new challenge, he was to me a typical English boy. By amazing coincidence, these three boys had all made their connections with their girlfriends, myself included, on the booze cruise in Nha Trang, Vietnam, and we ladies would continue to support their strong bonds of friendship and encourage their adventures together.

The plan was made for the three men to go on a big travel adventure together before we women tied them down and stole their time; they would travel in Africa for the entire six months. Stuart had already made contact with several individuals in the area and was looking into creating an animal sanctuary and rehabilitation centre in the middle of a Zambian national park, a space of land that was being offered for a reasonable price. After weeks of research, the decision was made for the boys to fly directly to Zimbabwe and then cross overland to Zambia, Botswana and Namibia.

In the meantime, I was going to return to Vancouver and work alongside one of Stuart's partners, trying to promote and sell trips for their travel company, the School of Travel Ltd. This would prove to be a challenge so soon after the events of 9/11 – the terrorist attack on the Twin Towers of the United States brought about an instant fear of travel. The fact that planes could be hijacked and used to kill innocent civilians put a different light on travelling, and trying to encourage travel at that time would become almost impossible.

I also had a big announcement to reveal to my Canadian family: during our last weeks together in England, Stuart had taken me on a beautifully prepared picnic on the hillside beside the sea and asked me if I would be his life partner, to make the commitment before we parted ways for the next six months. With a massive smile, I had accepted his proposal, and now wore the diamond ring that he had bought for me.

October was soon upon us and, as we parted ways, Stuart and I were happy with where life was taking us and grateful that we knew we would be coming back to each other. Stuart and the boys were off on an incredible backpacking expedition, while I was looking forward to some time at home with my family, an experience that I knew would not be as frequent in the years ahead.

Back home in Canada, I was delighted to be present for the birth of my elder sister's first child and was overjoyed to hear of the engagement of my best friend, Sarah. I experienced wonderful quality time with my family and friends within these months, and filled the days with mini adventures and expeditions, besides my work promoting the School of Travel. It was during this time that our wedding date was set, scheduled in the only month that fitted into our round-the-world travels, which unfortunately fell in the dreary and wet month of November.

The odd email from Stuart was now starting to find its way across the globe to me, and his handwritten letters of conquests and frustrations would reach me once a month. I started researching and creating a business plan for the Zambian animal sanctuary, trying to help the project by making it more professional and legitimate. Sadly, the red tape, bribes and backwards bureaucracy of the new Zambian government, which was keen to follow the misguided ways of the neighbouring Zimbabwean government of President Mugabe, kept the sanctuary from moving ahead. After months of his time, sweat and effort, Stuart had to let go of this dream, accepting that it would not come to fruition.

All was not lost; he now focused on enjoying his time with Tony and Duncan in Africa, including an opportunity to get extremely close to lions and cheetahs at a local rehabilitation centre. This experience took an unnerving turn when one of the lions appeared to become fixated on one of Stuart's sandals, then suddenly pounced, clenching its formidable jaws around Stu's foot. A keeper immediately grabbed hold of the lion's tail, pulling as hard as he could to try and drag it away, but it only tightened its grip. Soon, three keepers were at one end of the lion, all trying to wrench it away from Stuart. Everyone – especially Stuart – was very relieved when the lion let go without mangling his foot. The shoe didn't come off as lightly, but Stuart kept on wearing it for the rest of his time in Africa.

Another new focus was starting to gain significance. Stuart and I had met as two backpackers with independent lives and visions, and these would soon have to be altered to accommodate our union. Dreams of solitary travels within Africa were no longer realistic for Stuart, now that I was a permanent fixture in his life. The world would become our playground as we looked together at the infinite possibilities for adventure to come.

Chapter 6
The Legendary Glastonbury

Welcome back! Our reunion in England in April 2002 put Stuart and me back into a familiar way of life, and within a couple of weeks it felt like we had never been away. The only difference was the appearance of Stuart's brother Craig and his family, who had just moved from New Zealand to the UK. The two brothers now worked side by side, demonstrating 11 shows each day, including horse whispering, sheep racing and dog training.

Another change was the addition of Tony's girlfriend Adel, who had left her London life and moved in downstairs. The months passed quickly as our November wedding date grew closer and closer.

My time was being taken over by the South West Mountain Boarding Centre, a new business venture that Stu and I were setting up, together with Stu's boss from the tourist farm. Our aim was to use the mountain boards from Garry that Stuart had been unable to sell, as well as providing me with a paid job. I soon learned the technicalities of this sport that was so new to the UK and then became the main instructor, teaching young and old how to turn and sail safely down the sides of a grassy hill. Whenever I wasn't teaching mountain boarding, I applied myself to learning bookkeeping and accounting.

The Way of the Explorer

Our mountain-boarding venture was a success: a new sport had found its way to the slopes of the Devon coastline and a new group of individuals was coming together, creating a team that would one day compete in national- and world-level competitions. With this team, came Blue and his girlfriend Marci, who worked with Stuart at the tourist farm – two dynamic individuals that have remained close friends as our life unfolds. But not everything we did was based around work, and at the end of June we attended one of the most famous festivals in the world.

Growing up in Vancouver, I had enjoyed being in a city which hosted many world-famous musicians, my first concert being Michael Jackson's 'Bad' tour when I was 13. I loved seeing performances in all types of venues, but outside arenas that combined music with nature would become my favourite. I remember following the Dave Matthews Band around, attending six of their concerts, the best of which was a three-day event on the side of the Colorado River, in Gorge Washington. But nothing could have prepared me for the main event of the English summer season, an epic four-day concert where we were going to celebrate Stuart's 30th birthday. We had bought tickets for the legendary Glastonbury Festival.

I had never even heard about Glastonbury while in Canada, but would soon learn of its rich history. The festival was started in 1970 by a Somerset farmer, Michael Eavis, who had been influenced by hippie ethics and the free festival movement of the time. It covered all areas of the arts: contemporary music, dance, comedy, theatre, circus, cabaret and more. Each year the festival expanded to incorporate more stages and performance areas,

The Legendary Glastonbury

allowing alternative musicians to perform. The volume of attendees also increased, sometimes overrun by gatecrashers, bringing the total number to over 200,000. All of the festival goers, from performers and crew to paying attendees, would stay in tents, caravans or (the lucky ones) in motor homes. This meant that we had to be smart with our packing – everything had to be carried from the car park to the camping grounds, which in some cases took over an hour to walk to.

Stuart had mentioned his illegal attendance at this festival two years earlier, when he and two of his mates had hidden in the back of an empty diesel container and, while waiting for the best moment to escape and join the festivities, had nearly been overcome by the toxic fumes. It was this same festival that had been swamped by thousands of other illegal gatecrashers, causing it to be cancelled, with a one-million pound fine, the following year (2001) in order to address concerns over security and safety for the legitimate festival goers.

With the festival back on and the six days of work scheduled off, we packed our bags and stuffed our car. We decided to go to the site a day before the music began, wanting to find the best spot for our tent and an area large enough to accommodate ourselves and our best mates, Tony, Duncan and his girlfriend Wendy. We had also added two other friends to the mix, our fellow kindred spirits whom we had met in Devon, Marci and Blue.

The security of the site was impressive from the moment we entered, including a 10-foot steel fence circumventing the festival grounds. As we walked across the farmland, burdened by bags, we could see and hear the helicopters flying above, watching for any individual who tried to dig under or scale the perimeter barriers. And then you could see it: the Pyramid Stage, one of the main performance areas, 100 feet high and clad in dazzling silver. This is where we wanted to be. We scoped the camping area until we found the ultimate space, an area where we could see the main stage from the comfort of our tent as well as being framed off from the rest of the festival goers by the natural bush hedge.

The following days would be some of the best of my life as we danced to famous acts, including Stereophonics, Coldplay, Manu Chao, Rolf Harris, Fat Boy Slim, Rod Stewart, White Stripes and Faithless (and so many more). We weaved our way through the crowds to reach the dance tents and, smiling from ear to ear, we pulsed to the rhythms that were shaking the floors, so happy to be alive and to be experiencing the electrifying energy that surrounded us. We celebrated Stuart's big day, his 30th birthday, and felt blessed to be a part of this group of friends and with one another. We were creating memories and friendships that would last a lifetime.

We returned home to our cosy upstairs rooms, taking in the sense of peace and harmony in our well-being after such an epic festival, but within a few days our focus was once again drawn to the daily grind of work, and our evenings filled with practice. The new South West Mountain Boarding team was on the scene, made up of young men who were keen to race headlong down the steepest slopes, pushing the boundaries of this new sport. Most weekends found us at the top of the hill, sharing beer, and burgers cooked over a Kiwi-style barbecue, and laughing as we watched our boys sail through the air, egging each other on to go bigger and faster.

In August I returned to Vancouver and spent several weeks up on Pasley Island, enjoying the time I had with my best friend and my family, as we drank ciders on the dock and swam in the cool waters of the Pacific. And I busied myself in finalising plans and securing the food, flowers and music for my big day in November. When I had been back in Canada a few months earlier, I had decided on the date, venue, guest list and all other details of our wedding; my parents had very kindly offered to host the party in Canada rather than us getting married in New Zealand, far away from my large family clan.

I returned to England refreshed and reenergised, secure in the love of my family and friends, and looking forward to what lay ahead. Before setting off to Canada for the big event, Stuart took me to Germany for the first time, where I would meet his daughter. Marie was a beautiful baby girl who had been six months old when Stu and I first met in Vietnam.

Kirsten and Stuart had met in Australia and enjoyed each other's company enough to travel together in the outback. One starry night, feeling a close connection to the universe, they created a gift of life; a present to a woman who had always dreamed of having a child but thought she never could. This lovely lady, who was ten years my senior, was mature and wise enough to realise that it was smarter to raise the child on her own, and returned to Germany on her own with the intention of being a single mother. Stuart was given the choice either to stay connected to the child, or to end the relationship cleanly and forever. With love in his heart, he began the process of creating a relationship with his daughter to last a lifetime. So it was with this background that I would meet and begin my connection with Stuart's ex and their progeny.

The time came for our European adventures to end and, with promises of our next visit, we set off to Vancouver. We had no idea that the biggest test was yet to come.

Chapter 7
For Better or for Worse

Are there any weddings that go off without a hitch? I'm not too sure of the answer to that question, but what I do know is that Stuart and I were given three challenges before we said 'I do'. These tests would rock my foundations to the core and make me question whether I knew what I was doing, whether I had chosen the right man, and whether my family was supporting me unconditionally in the way I thought they should.

The first challenge started with my grandmother, a lovely, senior lady of 88, who was set in her ways and had had quite the life of adventures in her own right. But I remember her clutching her heart as Tony, one of Stuart's best men in the wedding party, walked into our wedding reception party, which my godmother and her husband, one of the Supreme Judges of BC, were hosting for us. As the long-haired hippy walking into the house, and with the kids screaming 'There's a street person in the house!', my grandmother fell back into the sofa and declared, 'I should be dead. I should be dead!' I had to run to reassure her and explain that this man was in fact Stuart's best friend, not someone off the street coming to gatecrash our party, and then had to continue my explanations as Stuart's second best man walked in – my granny had never seen a skinhead before. After I had placated her for several minutes, she seemed to accept the new arrivals, and she became more comfortable after meeting Tony and Duncan's other halves – Adel and Wendy had also flown over from the UK for the wedding.

The main challenge from my grandmother came later, after we had spent an evening with her in her home. I had taken Stuart to my granny's place in the hope of creating a bond between my man and the matriarch of our family, and soon felt we were on the right path. In this spirit, Stuart asked if we could borrow a photo of me, a professional one taken years earlier that stood on her mantelpiece beside the other photos of her grandchildren. We were creating a 'photo room' for our wedding, a room that was to be filled with images from Stuart's life and my own, and then a collage of photos from our time together. With the permission of my grandmother, we took the photo, not expecting the backlash that would follow.

We were enjoying a lovely, sociable evening with my best friend and maid of honour, Sarah, when I received an unexpected phone call from my dad. He was calling to let me know that my granny was phoning all of our extended family, telling them all that Stuart was a 'thief and a robber', that he had stolen a photo straight from under her nose. Due to her age, she had forgotten that she had given us permission to take it, and she was now planting seeds of negativity against my groom-to-be. I phoned her immediately to set the record straight, but I could hear in her voice that she still had her doubts and was troubled by the event. After many minutes of persuading her to see reason, she agreed to call back everyone she had phoned and explain that she had been mistaken.

Our next challenge came from my younger sister, Sasha. I have three sisters, one older and two younger, and because of the group dynamics and age, we would generally split into two camps: the older two and the younger two. As we entered the house on this day, I was verbally attacked by Sasha the minute I walked in the door with

Stuart. Having grown up with her, I had grown used to her outbursts. Unfortunately, Stuart had not, and, wanting to protect me, he talked back to her in a way she was not accustomed to. The two of them got into a very heated argument and, when it was over, Sasha fled from our parents' house, with daggers in her eyes and keys in hand. My youngest sibling, Ali, with her lifetime of experience in dealing with this sister, was sent on the search and found Sasha down on the beach, sitting on a log in the dark and watching the waves crash on the sand. The two girls returned to the house, after trying to explain Sasha's behaviour over hours of conversation, and a truce was made between Sasha and my husband-to-be. The wedding was still on.

The final test was the biggest, as it came from my father. Two days before the wedding, my dad asked me to come upstairs to his office so we could have a chat alone. I was not prepared for the words that came from his mouth; he stated that he didn't believe our marriage would last for more than five years and that he thought Stuart was a rough diamond. A rough diamond? His meaning was that Stuart was too rough around the edges. He questioned whether I had really thought this through and whether I really knew Stuart as I thought I did. I was mentally and emotionally floored by this attack and burst into tears as I just sat listening to my dad while he explained that he felt it was necessary to tell me his opinion before the big day.

After what seemed like an eternity, I left my dad's office broken-hearted to return downstairs to my bedroom, where I continued to cry into my pillow. I had passed Stuart on the stairs and, as he looked at me with concern, I couldn't find the words to explain my conversation with my dad. I didn't need to – my father asked Stuart up to his office to have the same talk. As with most parents, I had set

The Way of the Explorer

my dad up on a pedestal as the one who always knew best, but at this point could not understand how he could say what he did, two days before the wedding, saying that he had only my best interests in mind. Thoughts reeled through my head – probing, questioning, doubting – all trying to come to the best answer. Did I really know Stuart as I thought I did? Was I making the right decision? What should I do?

When Stuart finally joined me, he was furious. How dare my father make such statements and opinions days before the wedding! Stuart's family had been loving and accepting the moment they had heard of our engagement, and he was dumbfounded by the lack of welcome he had received from their Canadian counterparts. With my grandmother's accusations, my sister's attack and my father's five-year time limit to our marriage, Stuart couldn't understand why my family had not just accepted my decision and supported our union. But this was the test, the final exam before the graduation. Would we stay together or be swamped under by the negativity that was washing over us, letting go of our connection due to the forces around us?

My tears were present until the morning of the wedding, but my resolve was clear. I loved Stuart Barnes and I wanted to be with this man for the rest of my life. My other family members – my mum, my sisters Weeze and Ali, Margot (my cousin and travel companion), and my best friends Sarah and Amber – all rallied around me and Stuart. They gave us their support and encouragement, and tried to explain Dad's behaviour as that of someone who just didn't want to let me go. After the wedding I would not be returning to live in Canada, and they said he was afraid that he wouldn't see me often enough, that he would miss my presence. Being the second born, I had always been placed in the position of referee. I could get along with everybody and could calm situations down when things were boiling over, and had been able to smooth over many confrontations within the immediate family. With my absence, this role would be missing and this was making my dad nervous. My father was the emotional one of my parents, and he could not hide his tears and his feeling of loss from the rest of the family in the days leading up to our wedding.

The day before the wedding, I left to spend the night at my best friend's place and was spoilt by delectable treats and champagne, while she refuelled my spirit with her sound advice and counsel. I became excited again about the thought of joining Stuart for life, knowing in my heart of hearts that he was the man who could complete me. I was ready to be his wife. Finally, the moment came for our union, and as the priest from the Unitarian Church read out our vows and the Tibetan gong sounded, we looked into each other's eyes and made our commitment to each other. We were making a pact to love, support and cherish one another until death were to part us. We had passed our test. We knew that our future held infinite possibilities, and we knew that we would make the most of our time together, exploring the world while finding our inner strengths and our life purpose.

Our friends and family celebrated with us far into the night. Stuart and I looked forward to the next events to unfold, the first main event being a week away up at Pasley Island with the 18 individuals that had crossed oceans to be at our sides for our wedding. Bags were packed, food was organised and, with supplies of every sort stuffed into boxes, we all made the trek up to the island and enjoyed days of serenity and laughter, making the most of each other's company and the sanctuary of island life, as we watched the flames dance in the roaring fires and the waves crash against the shore.

Days raced past and it was soon time to embark on our honeymoon, a six-month adventure that was to take me to places I'd dreamed about as a child. Where was my future taking me? I wasn't sure on the end destination but I was looking forward to what lay in between, a life that I had never dreamed possible, one that would be filled with adventures that would make me question my personal beliefs and the beliefs of those who surrounded me.

With our marriage certificate packed safely away, Stuart and I boarded the plane with a light step, knowing that we had already overcome a major life challenge and that it had made us a stronger couple, forcing us to pull together and to believe in each other as we hadn't needed to in the past. We were ready to face the world and ride the wave of life, and we were excited about the journey ahead and everything that would come with it.

Chapter 8
Our Global Honeymoon

There was a gigantic piece of poo in the toilet. This is what set me off; I burst into tears just after we finally arrived at the first stop on our wedding tour. After days of travel, including two very scary plane rides as we were whipped around by crazy trade winds above the Pacific Ocean, and crowded bus rides and boat crossings, we had arrived at Leleuvia Island. I had booked for us to stay on this tiny Fijian island, a coral cay encased by white sands and turquoise waters. The island could be circumnavigated in a 30-minute walk and was a jewel within the South Pacific Sea. But all I could see was the large piece of faecal matter in our toilet as we entered our 'honeymoon suite'. This was NOT what I had ordered!

Stuart found me a strong drink and led me away to sit on the white sands (having flushed the toilet on his exit), and calmed me down with words that made me see the insignificance of the colossal poo against the beauty of where we were. Even though I had been initially disappointed by the bare, rustic wooden structure that was our honeymoon suite, I would grow to love this island and the family that owned it, sharing wonderful moments with them as we ate fresh fish each night and drank the local spirits.

The waters were full of colourful fish and we snorkelled for hours each day, then walked along the stunning beaches, holding hands and cherishing our new titles of Mr and Mrs Barnes. It was with sad hearts that we left our newfound friends a week later. We made our move to islands off the west coast of the main island, and it was here that we learned about the Fijian culture and the impact of foreign investment.

Our next port of call was an area that was experiencing a huge increase of tourists; the feel of the islands was changing as they moved from the hands of the native population to foreign management. New forms of transport were coming onto the scene, and instead of being on 'Fiji Time', where you could wait for hours for the departure of a vessel, we very soon found ourselves on a fast-moving speedboat that had replaced the traditional wooden dinghy. Boat crossings that used to take hours now took less than an hour, and new hotels and guesthouses under construction could be seen on the many islands we passed. We learned from our Fijian hosts that they were in talks with an Australian company that wanted to buy their resort, and they asked for our opinions on the matter. Delving further into the topic, we found out that the Fijians have a wonderful custom, where the families within each village contribute to the livelihood of all individuals of the village; money made by each family goes to the elders and is then evenly distributed to the rest of the clan. This meant that any profits our landlords were making was being spread out to help all the others within their group.

As we drank the traditional 'cava' and listened to the depressing stories of development on neighbouring islands, we tried to dissuade our host from selling up for the instant gratification of a lump sum of money, to make him realise the long-term ramification of selling off his main resource: his land. Once the money had been spent, we reasoned, the village people would have very limited resources in order to continue to grow and survive. As the winds of change were clearly in the air, we prayed that he would find the wisdom and the strength to make the right choice, to preserve his land for his people and for future generations.

The stress of our wedding and everything that went with it became a distant memory as Stuart and I enjoyed the Fijian sun, the fresh food and the ocean waters. By the time our three weeks were up, we were ready for our next destination: New Zealand.

Stuart's family members were all present when we arrived at Christchurch airport and they welcomed us, the newly wedded couple, with open arms into their fold. We would spend Christmas all together, and I would experience the new tradition of having a 'barbie' (barbecue) in shorts and singlets on December 25th. This was a complete contrast to my previous Christmases, where a roaring fire and blaring carols were the norm. In the weeks that followed, Stu and I were treated to a hot-air balloon safari over the Canterbury Plains of New Zealand. We were lucky enough to receive a one-day window in which the bad weather cleared and the grey skies disappeared, allowing us to go up thousands of feet in the small wooden basket. There everything grew silent, except for the odd blast of gas to help our ascent. We could see the layout of the land below, tiny little boxes that represented the farmland borders. This was a new experience for both of us and, holding hands, we rejoiced in our present and future adventures together.

I later travelled alone to the west coast of the island, staying with my 'New Zealand sister', Gina, the girl I had worked and lived with a few years earlier, while Stuart spent a few days alone with his mother, exploring his native island. The highlight of my visit was when a good friend of Gina's took me on a helicopter tour to explore the majestic Mount Cook. I couldn't believe my luck as I sat there in the front passenger seat, spellbound as we flew up Fox Glacier, appreciating the spectacularly rugged beauty as we crossed over deep crevices and uncovered, sky-blue ice formations. The Southern Alps were stunning, with their hanging glaciers, vast snowfields and monumental mountains, and I was blown away when it came to our snow landing on Mount Cook's alpine ridge. I felt completely in awe of nature and the universe, and felt a heightened sense of self, a connection to this planet as never before, and I counted my blessings. Stuart and his mum met me on my return, and they both had to smile when they saw the condition I was in; I was completely overwhelmed by my complimentary helicopter experience and would be on a high for days.

Our next port of call was Australia. Stuart's sister, Louise, had gifted us a week's trip to the Sunshine Coast, Queensland, where her family of four and the two of us would stay in a beautiful resort near many of the tourist attractions in the area. We enjoyed great days out at Steve Irwin's Australian Zoo, holding koala bears and giant pythons, then returned to our resort to swim in the massive pool and drink margarita cocktails at the poolside. Many laughs were shared and the days passed too quickly before we were all at the airport again, with the west coast of this massive country as our next destination.

We were met at Perth Airport by Stuart's uncle, Rob, a legendary figure who was extremely close to my husband and who welcomed us with a warm hug and a large joint. We laughed our way down the coast before arriving at his farm, which overlooked the Atlantic

Ocean. From there we could see kangaroos hopping across the land and hear the calls of the kookaburra. Rob had a vision of creating a self-contained kibbutz, a place where you could survive off the land, with 'No Worries' as his motto and the name of the community. On most days I could see the two men working together on one of the farm's machines or fixing a fence line, very happy just to be in each other's company. Then we'd all go down to Greens Pool, an extraordinarily beautiful beach with clear emerald waters, pure white sands, and sculpted rocks that sheltered the bay from the swell beyond. In the weeks that followed, I would meet Stuart's extended family – his mum had come from this area – and get to know his grandmother, two aunts and two uncles, as well as all their relations. My family was growing.

It should be mentioned at this point that we were constantly being questioned about the direction of our future, with the most common enquiry about when we were planning on having children. Having just embarked on a new and exciting lifestyle, alternating work and exploration, I didn't feel kids came into the picture, and I started to sense that they might never be a feature in our lives. This was a major self-revelation, but I was having too much fun in our adventures and growing so much in myself that I felt it was alright to be selfish – children would change everything. I loved our time and did not want to change it.

Our next destination was one I had dreamed about since I was a little girl: Africa. I remember being in the sixth grade and seeing 45-second adverts on TV of the famines that had struck Ethiopia, showing young black children with flies crawling over their eyes and nostrils, and with stomachs bloated due to malnutrition, scenes that made me burst into tears because of the injustice of it all. In fact, if my older sister was mad at me for something, she'd find and play those commercials just so she could see me fall apart at the seams. Those visual images would not leave my head, and seeing my fellow classmates throwing away perfectly good food at lunchtime spurred me to write a strong letter to the principal of my elementary school, questioning him on what he was doing to better the lives of our fellow human beings. I thought I was going to be in big trouble when I was called to the principal's office, and was surprised when he challenged me to represent our school at a City Hall meeting, where African delegates were discussing the issues of their land and what we could do to help. After attending the meeting I came up with a fundraising idea of a 'spell-a-thon', and our school raised over $7,000 to be sent to aid the suffering country. I learned of Africa's struggles, from its history of wars and injustices to its natural disasters of droughts and floods, and also became aware of the uniqueness of its wildlife, both on the land and in the water. This knowledge stuck with me, making me dream of one day visiting Africa.

So we were off, flying from Perth to Johannesburg, South Africa, where we barely touched down before flying to Windhoek, Namibia. Namibia was known to be a politically stable country that was much safer than its southerly neighbour, and an easy transition for a girl who'd never set foot on African soil. Since Stuart had explored this continent on his own on several occasions, I gave him the reins to plan our tour and was happy to sit back and see where we ended up. We rented a car and drove north, where I was surprised by the well-maintained roads and the infrastructure of the country. We stopped several times at well-maintained service stations and found the route easy to follow. Our first stop was Etosha National Park, a 22,000 square kilometre, malaria-free area that boasted endangered black rhinos, lions, cheetahs, elephants and zebras, as well as a 5,000 square kilometre salt pan that attracted thousands of flamingos. I immediately fell in love with this wilderness, taking photo after photo, swinging my camera from one animal to the next, blown away by the proximity of these wild beasts.

We spent ten days in the park and were always among the first to leave the secured campground at sunrise and often the last to return, just before the campground gates were shut at sundown. We'd plan our day's expedition, using the map to choose new routes so that we could cover as much ground as possible. Then we'd return in the evening to jump in the pool before retiring to our tent, going over the thousands of digital photos taken that day and making space on the memory card for the next day's adventures.

On one of the evenings we went to one of the floodlit waterholes for night-time game viewing. It was here that we would tune into our inner voices, an action that possibly saved our lives. We had been sitting for several minutes on a terraced seating area, watching the rhinos approach the waterhole below, when Stuart looked at me and said that we needed to move, 'Now!' Nothing I could see would give away the reason for this command but, following Stuart's intuition, we moved up three terrace levels and over by about 30 feet, calmly sitting back down to continue to watch the scene below. Less than two minutes later we watched a very large black mamba, one of the most feared and deadliest snakes of Africa, come out of the scrub from above and cross over the area where we had been sitting. I thanked God that I had listened and followed Stuart's lead – we would not have seen the highly venomous snake as it slithered down the steps from behind where we had been sitting. We left the area shortly afterwards, cautiously scanning the path with our flashlight, thinking of the 'what if' scenario had we stayed in our original spot.

This incident made me flashback to the time when I had travelled to Florida with my boyfriend in my early 20s. We had made a day trip to an uninhabited island off the coast known for its great hiking trails, but which also held the caution to be on the lookout for the dangerous diamondback rattlesnake. The poisonous rattlesnake bite was extremely painful and can be fatal – the warning signs at the entrance to the walk stated that you would have only a couple of hours to get help, before the poison took over your body. Not expecting to see anything dangerous, we had followed the arrows and started our walk and were halfway across the island when it happened. We had been walking hand in hand along the path when we turned a corner, and there it was ... a massive, seven-foot diamondback rattlesnake, as thick as my thigh, coiled up in the centre of the path, looking ready to strike. We stopped dead in our tracks and, as the snake's head weaved back and forth and the tail rattled loudly, my boyfriend turned to me and said 'Don't move.' It must have been a complete shock to him when he turned to find I'd already disappeared – I had hightailed it out of there as quickly as my shaking legs would take me. With this memory resurfacing, I thanked God I did not have to face a black mamba on that star-filled night; going on my past experience, I don't know if I'd have managed to remain motionless.

Another major event was to occur one evening within the grounds of the National Park, one that would give Stuart a sleepless night while I lay beside him, trying to find my dreamland. A major storm was on its way, and it was the first time I had ever seen such an enormous mushroom cloud on the horizon. We battened down the tent and secured our gear in the car, waiting for the storm to arrive. Earlier that day we had chosen a tent site under the one and only tree within this deserted area, trying to find shade from the soaring daytime heat, and we were sheltering again under the tent flaps when the first rain appeared.

At first we were thankful to be under the tree, with some protection from the lashing showers, but Stuart's concern grew as the sheet and forked lightning grew closer and closer. He was acutely aware that we had placed ourselves under the tallest structure in the deserted campground and that our tent was held together by steel rods. The rains grew harder, the wind shook our tent and Stuart sat at the entrance to the tent, rocking himself with worry, trying to decide whether we should leave our dwelling or stay in its shelter. At one point he poked me and pointed to a branch not even ten feet above us. There sat a serval, an African wildcat, which was obviously on the lookout for some shelter from the electrifying weather that was engulfing the savannahs. Within the next few minutes we watched this wildcat as it came closer to us, finally finding shelter in the area just inside our exterior tent flap.

Stuart continued to count the seconds between lightning strikes and, as the massive mushroom cloud sat directly above us, lightning strikes started to come in two-second intervals. It was at this point that Stuart made the decision that we needed to evacuate our potentially dangerous site. We ran to our car and drove a few miles away, believing it was safer to be in a vehicle with four rubber tyres that might prevent an electrical current from grounding itself. We waited just under an hour before the storm passed and we could return to camp, finding the comfort of our sleeping bags and leaving the stress of the storm behind us.

With many wildlife encounters under our belts, we left the Etosha National Park in the north-east of the country and drove south-west, entering the Namib Desert and its northern coastline, which is referred to as the 'Skeleton Coast'. Considered to be the oldest desert in the world, this two-million hectare area is one of the most inhospitable and least visited places on Earth. As we drove down the paved road into the desert I watched rugged canyons, with their walls of richly coloured volcanic rock, and the extensive mountain range give way to flat plains and windswept dunes. At last, we arrived in the coastal town of Swakopmund. The town is sandwiched between the cold breakers of the South Atlantic and the burning heat of the desert. As we enjoyed a cold beer, I was surprised by our surroundings; the whitewashed and half-timbered buildings reminded me of the architecture I had seen in southern England. It was here that I would learn about the history of the area, including why the northern Namibian coastline had been named the Skeleton Coast. There had been a number of famous shipwrecks on its shores, which had led to many sailors perishing as they walked for hundreds of kilometres through the barren landscape in search of food and water. In addition to the bones left by the stranded sailors, the name also comes from the other bones that now line the beaches, from whaling operations and seal hunts.

We made daily trips to the surrounding areas, using our map to guide us along deserted roads. On one trip we explored the ghost town of Kolmanskop, once a small but very rich diamond-mining village, which had declined after World War I when the diamond field was exhausted. The German government had claimed the area when one of its railroad workers had discovered a diamond, and had immediately built a German-style village to accommodate the rapid influx of miners. In the town there had been a hospital, ballroom, power station, school, skittle alley, theatre, sports hall, casino, ice factory, and the first x-ray station in the Southern Hemisphere as well as the first tram in Africa. Less than half a century later we walked amongst the ruins, shuffling our way through the houses, which were knee-deep in sand; the surrounding desert sands had reclaimed the space as their own.

Another day trip took us to Deadvlei, an area that had once been a marsh but was now a dried, white clay pan, surrounded by some of the highest sand dunes in the world. These dunes have literally rusted over thousands of years, giving them a fiery complexion. The ancient marsh had been home to camel thorn trees, but when the climate changed a thousand years ago and drought struck the area, the water supplies were cut off and the trees were unable to survive. Fortunately the trees did not disappear; the climate was so harsh that the trees dried out instead of decomposing, and the desert sun scorched them into blackened bones, never to vanish from the earth. So there we were, walking amongst 900-year-old tree skeletons, with a background of red, rusted dunes and a brilliant blue sky: a forest frozen in time.

Our last stop within Namibia would take us back to the east coast, to a game reserve which held the wild dogs of Africa and where Stuart had worked as a volunteer in previous years. This would be my first experience with these rare and highly intelligent canines and I watched in awe as they devoured a kudu, the second largest antelope

The Way of the Explorer

in the world, ripping it to shreds within minutes, with squeals of excitement. It was here that I would pet my first cheetah, which the owners of the game reserve had raised since a cub, and where I would get up close and personal to large male lions and leopards. These close encounters would be a highlight of my Namibian travels, and I looked forward to a time when I could experience them all over again.

With so many countries to explore and with time against us, we returned our rental car to the capital and hopped on a bus, with Livingstone, Zambia, as our next destination. I had to be forewarned about our journey – we would be driving through the Caprivi Strip, a small region of conflict nestled between Namibia, Botswana and Angola. Both the Namibian military and a small gang of rebels were attempting to claim the Caprivi Strip as their own, resulting in deadly clashes throughout the 1990s. This was the main trade route linking landlocked Zambia and neighbouring countries, such as DR Congo, Malawi and Zimbabwe, to the Atlantic Ocean, and armed military convoys were present to escort vehicles twice a day through the region. This would be another first for me, to be chaperoned by jeeps with massive swivel guns extending over their front bonnets. Then my anxieties turned to wonder as we drove through Chobe National Park, Botswana's famous game reserve, watching as elephants strolled casually past our bus windows.

The day passed quickly as Stuart recounted hilarious stories, describing his last year's adventures while he worked at one of the game reserves along the Caprivi Strip. His job was taking the young men and women from the 'Overlander' trucks out on boats to view wildlife. On many occasions, as he neared the hippos – some of the most dangerous animals in all of Africa – in the river, he would describe the specific body language that signalled that the animals were feeling threatened and when they might charge to defend themselves. Then, with the scene set, Stuart would play his trick. Stopping a safe distance from the hippos, he would tell tales about how fast they could charge and, when nobody was looking, would purposely switch the boat's engine lever to 'off'. As the guests watched nervously, Stuart would make several attempts at pulling the pull start cord, anxiously watching the waters, increasing the tension in the air. The boat would drift closer to the animals and, as the nervousness turned to panic, Stuart would suddenly switch the lever back to 'on' and start the engine. The group would be led safely away, often back to the campground bar, where they would laugh over their day's adventures and buy Stuart many drinks for getting them out of the dangerous situation.

We crossed two border points on our full day of travel, exiting Namibia, crossing through the northern tip of Botswana, and then finally moving on to Zambia. The town of Livingstone was home to 'Jollyboys Backpackers', a hostel that Stuart knew very well. It was run by two lively and wonderful girls, Kim and Sue, who welcomed us into their home and allowed us to stay free of charge in the newly built annexe. We were thankful for the homey feel of it all and to be surrounded by friendly faces, especially when Stu fell ill with malaria for the third time in his life. I felt really daunted when we received confirmation of the illness from the health centre in town. I was aware of the statistics: malaria had killed up to half of all the people that ever lived in this world, and there are up to half a billion cases every year, leading to around two million deaths. Not an encouraging prospect. But Stuart was calm, taking everything in his stride and assuring me that the key was just to catch the illness in the early stages. His first experience with malaria had been in Malawi in 1995, when the illness progressed to a stage where, although conscious, he had been unable to move from his bed or even make a sound when two individuals came into his room and stole most of his belongings. It was only thanks to two fellow Kiwis that he had survived. They had heard of the sick 'mzungu' – a term used for 'white person' in Africa – and had dragged him from his hut and brought him to the hospital in Harare. It took him a couple of weeks to recover fully from that episode, but it gave him the experience to recognise the symptoms and to react more quickly in the case of future attacks. So his strength returned within a few days this time, and he was soon ready to show me the sights of the area.

Our first stop would be one of the world's seven natural wonders, the Victoria Falls. With cameras packed, we made our way to the Victoria Falls National Park. Even from miles away from the entrance to the park I could see a massive column of mist in the air, signalling the location of the majestic falls, and I counted down the minutes until our arrival with anticipation. Nothing could have prepared me for what we were about to witness – a spectacular sight of super-natural beauty that took my breath away and captivated my soul.

We stood beside this natural wonder, classified as the largest waterfall in the world due to the enormous volumes of falling water. We took photos as the water thundered down a vertical drop of 100 metres, transforming the Zambezi from a placid river into a ferocious torrent as it cut through a series of dramatic gorges. The width of the falls is almost two kilometres, and I held my breath as I watched Stu wade out across the top ridge of the river, knowing that one wrong step could cause his death; no human (or animal) could survive a trip over the falls.

I was thankful to have been prewarned about the moisture in the air, having protected my camera from the tremendous spray that shot upwards like inverted rain, as we walked along a path on the edge of the forest and then carefully crossed the knife-edge bridge. We took in the spectacular views of the eastern cataract and up the main gorge; I had never seen such awe-inspiring beauty, nor been deafened by the power of nature before, and I marvelled at the perfection of this planet.

We made our way along the various paths on-site, and came upon a memorial of Dr David Livingstone, where I learned of his influence in the area. He was noted to be the first European to see and publicise the falls, naming his discovery in honour of Queen Victoria, and this in turn had opened up Central Africa to other missionaries, hunters and traders. He made significant contributions to medicine, geography and natural history, and his experiences in Africa led him to become a leading anti-slavery crusader. The town closest to the falls would be named in his honour and it is his description of this natural wonder that lives on in prosperity. He wrote, 'No one can imagine the beauty of the view from anything witnessed in England. It had never been seen before by European eyes; but scenes so lovely must have been gazed upon by angels in their flight.' Witnessing the falls with my own eyes, I completely agreed with his description.

We left the town of Livingstone after a few weeks, heading to the capital of Zambia, Lusaka, then on to Harare. I was excited about visiting the capital of Zimbabwe, especially after hearing Stuart's stories of his time there in 1995, and could envision the multicultural society, the modern city life and the westernised shopping malls. Moving from the relaxed and slow-moving pace of life in Zambia, where our diet had been very limited, I was surprised by how appealing a McDonald's or Pizza Hut menu suddenly seemed. And it would feel reassuring to encounter more Westerners – I'd felt as if I stuck out like a sore thumb, with my blonde hair and blue eyes, living among mostly African natives for such a long time.

Stuart warned me that things had changed for the worse since he'd last been there, but even he was shocked as we entered Harare – the city was almost unrecognisable. This had once been one of his favourite cities in Africa, but the people had changed; there was no longer a multicultural feel to the city, and the energy in the air was one of survival. We witnessed queues that went on for miles, where people were desperately trying to buy the limited fuel that was available in only a few of the operational service stations, since President Robert Mugabe had stopped paying other countries for basic supplies. The people were suffering while Mugabe lived like a king, and this was evident all around us.

After what seemed like ages, our taxi driver drove us to the one and only hostel in the area that was open. We were relieved to be off the streets and welcomed into a lovely house by a fifth-generation white Zimbabwean woman, our hostess for the next few nights. It was here that we would learn about the deterioration of the country and the desperation of its people, and I was shocked by the human struggle for survival, due largely to their president.

Robert Mugabe had been elected prime minister in 1980, the year of independence from British rule, and later became president of Zimbabwe. The country had once been known to be so rich in agricultural produce that it was dubbed the 'bread basket' of Southern Africa. Now, after two decades of rule, Zimbabwe was at a low point in its history. The poverty situation was in an extreme stage, since Mugabe had encouraged the takeover of white-owned commercial farms. This 'fast-track resettlement program' had led to the economic collapse of the nation and to runaway inflation. The white farmers were forced off their lands, often together with their farm workers, resulting in soaring unemployment rates as workers and their dependent families – millions of individuals – lost their livelihoods. We were told horrifying tales of obscene violence as white farmers were forced to leave their properties, leaving them with absolutely nothing – they were never compensated for their land. And their workers were excluded from redistribution, at the same time as losing their jobs on the farms.

I learned how the Zimbabwean people were struggling to survive. Once a wealthy country with surplus agricultural product to sell to the rest of the world, Zimbabwe now struggled to feed its own population. The high unemployment rate, combined with a severe drought, extreme crop failure and the collapse of food production due to mismanagement, resulted in increased living costs that were causing the poverty situation to worsen to extreme levels. And this struggle was made real for us as we sat listening late into the evening to the stories from our host. She was in her 60s and, pointing to her packed bags in the corner of the room, she explained how she was ready to flee her home at a moment's notice. This was a place that had been a part of her family history for five generations.

We consulted our host's knowledge of the city as we asked for her opinion on the best places to visit; we had seen no other tourist when we drove through the city streets and assumed most tourist attractions would be shut down. She guided us to a wildlife sanctuary only a few miles from her home, where we came within a few metres of zebras, impalas, giraffes, wildebeest, elands and crocodiles as we rode horseback through the reserve. To top it all off, with us being the only visitors to the centre that month, we were given special treatment: we were brought into the enclosure where the young elephants lived and were allowed to feed the majestic animals by hand.

With a few hours to spare, we took a taxi to one of the only street markets still open and bought beautiful native paintings and wood carvings. Within minutes of being there we could feel the desperation in the air as all the stand holders tried to push their wares on us, selling intricate pieces of work for a fraction of the normal cost. With only minimal space left in our backpacks, we had to say 'no' to most sellers. As a result, we could soon feel their anger emanating towards us – tourists were seen to have surplus money and we were not sharing ours. We jumped back into our waiting taxi and left the market area, becoming ever more certain that we needed to leave this country as soon as possible. It wasn't a safe time to be here.

The following evening we took a taxi to the main railway station, knowing that there was a train leaving for the Mozambique border. Stuart prewarned me to take extra-special care in this very public place – we stood out like dollar signs to the locals and would be easy meal tickets to a desperate individual. Stuart made it clear to me that we had to appear very confident, and to show that we would put up a fight against those individuals that prayed on the weak. We kept our shoulders back and eyes up, staring back at those individuals who tried to challenge us. We bought our 'first-class sleeper car' tickets, legged it to our train and locked ourselves into our compartment, aware that we were being constantly watched and followed. We breathed a sigh of relief only when the train started to move down the tracks. Zimbabwe had changed from a place of growth and prosperity to a country of desperation and poverty, and I felt awful for every citizen within its borders.

It was the first time in my life that I was excited to see the custom control and immigration counters that signalled a border crossing, and I felt a huge weight leave my shoulders as we walked onto Mozambique soil. Even though we had heard stories of the internal clashes in the north and the high poverty rates, with more than 50 per cent of Mozambicans living on less than US$1 a day, we were grateful to be in this developing country, which incorporates one of the longest coastlines in all of Africa and has Portuguese as its official spoken language.

Our first task was to find transportation to take us south. With no buses in sight, Stuart began chatting with a fellow Caucasian who had just come across the border; he had an open-bed truck and was on his own. One thing that I was learning by watching Stuart, was that there are always opportunities around us, if you are open enough to see them. Within no time at all, we were comfortably seated in the back of his truck, taking in the scenery as we covered mile after mile, and I found myself digesting the fact that this was the first-ever hitchhiking experience my life. Having Stuart at my side gave me extra confidence to take on activities that had previously been outside my comfort zone, which in turn helped me to believe that I could conquer anything I set my mind to. He was an experienced explorer, with an amazing understanding of the animal kingdom, and I put my life in his hands as we enjoyed our six-month honeymoon, traversing the continent from shore to shore, soaking up all the wondrous scenery and experiences that we encountered.

We had been travelling for most of the day when our ride slowed to a stop behind a line-up of vehicles on the hot, tar-sealed road. Our path was being blocked, not by passing livestock or police cordons, but by a massive amount of water, a river that was flowing over the top of our road and which stretched out as far as the eye could see. No cars or trucks were moving into the water to attempt the crossing and, as our driver decided to abandon his journey and return north until the waters had receded, Stuart and I contemplated our next course of action. We walked to the front of the line of vehicles and I watched as Stuart scanned the various forms of transport there. Soon he focused in on a Toyota Hilux truck and moved in to join the discussion with the rest of the men. After several minutes he returned to say we were moving, jumping on the back of the Hilux as it was to be the first vehicle in a convoy to make an attempt to cross the waters – an only slightly preferable alternative to sleeping in our tent at the side of the road.

As the truck moved out into the water, Stuart instructed me to place all my critical documents on my person; I stuffed my passport, credit cards and money into my money belt, ready at his signal to abandon my pack and jump into the waters. He showed me where it would be safe to leap from in order to avoid getting in the way of our truck if it overturned, and he cautioned me on the severity of the crossing and what I should do if I was swept away downriver. We could see sections of the concrete from the road being whisked along by the ferocious torrent, and I prayed with every breath that we would make it safely to the other side. The water was flowing over the tops of our tyres and up the side of the cab, its current pushing us to the left. I could hear our driver swearing as he tried to stay on the road, pushing his vehicle against the force of the river. The vehicles behind us were also feeling the pressure and we signalled frantically for them to turn into the current as they were pushed to within centimetres of the sharp drop where the road had been washed away.

The crossing would be the most intense half-hour of my life; we readied ourselves a number of times to jump from the truck, and I prayed like I had never prayed before. I watched as we passed overturned trucks, their drivers sitting forlornly on top, victims of the natural elements who would have to wait until the water receded before they could get help. I thanked the good Lord that we were still moving and unharmed. And then it was over. We had made it over the river and were on our way south to the town of Maxixe in the Inhambane province, where we would say thank you and goodbye to our lift. We then found our way to Tofo, a small village on the coast of the Indian Ocean, where we could relax in beach huts and dive in some of the best waters in the world, known for their local whale sharks, manta rays and sea turtles.

The tension of the past week of travel melted away as we relaxed in the honeymoon suite in the Bamboozi resort, an amazing chalet built on the top of the dune, with views of the deep, turquoise sea in front and a coconut grove behind. The days rolled into weeks as we soaked up the chilled vibe and ate amazing seafood. After dives, where we swam within metres of the largest shark in the world, we made plans to return the following year for a season of work, with the goal of becoming certified as dive masters. We had become friends with Dez, the owner of Bamboozi, and agreed to his proposal for us to work for him for six months in exchange for our dive-master qualifications and all the certification that goes with it. We were excited about the future, and also wanted to make the most of our remaining time in Africa, so we eventually left the Bamboozi Beach Lodge and travelled south into South Africa, to a private property adjacent to the famous Kruger National Park. We had met a group of men while walking the beaches of Tofo and had been invited to join their rowdy group as they fished and drank beer. They had awarded me the captain's chair once they had heard that I had worked at a fishing lodge and it hadn't taken long before we were thrown invitations to see the best of their beloved South Africa. When Stuart had heard about Kevin's farm, with no fences or barriers to separate it from the massive Kruger Park, he had jumped at the opportunity.

We spent five days on Kevin's property and were spoiled by his local knowledge of the environment and by the home-cooked meals he prepared for us. Kevin had grown up on the farm, a massive section of land where the main focus was game viewing, and he knew the footprints of all the animals that crossed his lands. With a loaded shotgun slung over his shoulder, he took us on walks and showed us the evidence of the different creatures that roamed the grounds both day and night. Then we would jump into his open-top truck, which had no roof or sides and just the front pane of glass to view through, and go on tracking expeditions. One evening, in the pitch blackness, Kevin packed us up into the jeep, wanting us to experience a night-time game viewing. With headlights on full beam, he followed the animal tracks that he could see in the dust on the road, and we soon came upon a pride of lions feasting after a kill. Kevin brought the car to a stop in the centre of six lions, all red-faced with blood as they tore into a dead wildebeest. Their jaws snapped as they chomped away on the meat and bones, tearing their kill to shreds. I couldn't believe my eyes as we sat there in such an exposed position in the open-top jeep and I held my breath, hoping that the pride wouldn't take exception to their audience. Even though the shotgun was still present, leaning against Kevin's thigh, I felt that I could easily be the next meal ticket, and I stayed as still as possible, desperately trying not to attract the lions' attention. At one point Kevin turned off the headlights; in the pitch blackness all we could hear was the crunching of bones and the occasional roar of a lion. We stayed there for a good 20 minutes, admiring the raw beauty of the scene, before heading off into the bush to track down other large mammals, including four white rhinos at a watering hole.

The wildlife surrounding Kevin's home sometimes came a little too close for comfort. On one occasion the boys headed out to the outhouse, as someone had spotted a black mamba in a latrine and wanted to get rid of it. Having already learned about this deadly snake, I felt no need to participate in its evacuation and stayed safely indoors, anxiously awaiting the return of my brave husband and our host. After an hour with no success in finding the snake, Kevin decided to search for some of the park's other elusive animals. With our cameras ready we boarded the open-top jeep and made our way out into the bush, following the dirt roads.

I could tell something had grabbed Kevin's attention as he scanned the track, and it wasn't long before he parked up under a tree, pointing for us to look up. Oh my God! There was a massive male leopard on the branch above our heads! At first I couldn't believe it, thinking it must be the trick of the sunlight as the animal made its way through the branches. But as my eyes adjusted to the shadowy lighting, his huge frame became clear and I raised my camera to get a shot of the magnificent beast. It was at this point that he moved, rushing down the branch towards us and coming to within ten feet of where we sat, baring his teeth as he snarled at us. I was aware of the idea that an animal would think we were part of the vehicle if we sat motionless inside, but I wasn't sure if this applied when the animal stood right above us, and I felt completely exposed and at his mercy.

With a smile on his face, Kevin slowly put the jeep into reverse, calmly talking about the bluffed charge we had just witnessed, as if it was something he had seen a hundred times. His knowledge of his land and of the animals in the wild would be our fortune; time and again he brought us into close proximity with the game life, allowing us to witness the African animals in their natural setting. When our time was up we thanked our host for the amazing experiences he had given us, and looked forward to seeing what we could find on our own. We now prepared ourselves for our last big safari, a week inside the famous Kruger National Park.

We picked up our rental car and arrived at the gates of the park, excited about the days ahead. This park was known for having the 'Big Five' game animals, as well as more species of large mammals than any other African Game Reserve. These included wild dogs, and we scanned the landscape as soon as we entered the park, cameras ready to document our sightings. Every day brought new sightings, from lions, cheetahs, leopards and cape buffalo to the endangered black rhino, but one event stood out from all the others, testing Stuart's animal sense to the extreme.

Stuart had been driving our little Suzuki hatchback for most of the morning when we came upon a large male elephant in front of us on the road, a beautiful animal with massive ivory tusks. In my experience, elephants would generally move into the bush when they saw a vehicle approaching, but this one had a different agenda; it blocked our path, moving towards us, its trunk swaying ominously from side to side. As ours was the only vehicle on the road and with nowhere to turn, with wooded brush on one side and a ravine on the other, Stuart put the car into reverse and we backed away from the oncoming mammal. We continued to reverse as the bull elephant charged us, picking up speed in intervals as it trumpeted and flicked its ears. We were forced to signal to a jeep that arrived on the scene to back up and get out of our way.

After three kilometres of reversing, Stuart had had enough and decided it was time to change his tactics. He explained that he could see signs the elephant was tiring, so instead of backing up he now stopped our vehicle in the road, waiting for the animal's next move. The elephant approached us slowly and came within a few metres of our car, then stopped to have a look at the bush. And this is when Stuart took his chance. Slamming the manual transmission into second gear, he manoeuvred our car into the tight space between the bull elephant and the ravine, surprising the animal by moving forwards instead of backwards. He skirted around the side of the great beast and only narrowly escaped the path of the swinging tusks as the elephant tried to push our vehicle down the embankment. We had been so close to the wild beast that I could see his individual eyelashes as we passed and I couldn't believe Stuart had challenged him in this way. What if the rental car had not changed gears as quickly as he had hoped?! After a few choice words, I calmed down enough to hear Stuart's explanation of animal behaviour, and within a few minutes felt exhilarated by the experience.

Our six-month honeymoon was coming to an end. As I scanned through all the photos we had taken, I felt humbled by my new life of adventure, with the freedom to go where I chose, and with an experienced explorer at my side. The future held infinite possibilities for adventure and I thanked the universe for guiding me to Stuart, for keeping us safe along our journey and for guiding us on our choices for future expeditions.

The world is a book and those who do not travel read only one page.

Augustine of Hippo

Chapter 9
Mountain-boarding and Mozambique

How is it that, after six months of exploring the world and experiencing amazing new adventures, we could return to work in the UK and within a couple of weeks feel like we'd never left?

The memories of our recent exploits were receding to the back of my mind, replaced by the demands of our mountain-boarding centre. We had run an advertisement in the local newspaper to say that we would be open during the two-week Easter break, and we now had very little time left to get the equipment and the course ready. My daylight hours saw me combing the tracks, removing any rocks or debris that could get in the way of the riders, trying to make the extreme sport as safe as possible. This recreational pastime was starting to increase in popularity and riders were arriving from all over the country, wanting to try out our new centre with its assorted tracks and jumping area.

It was at this time that we were approached by one of the main board manufacturers and, after numerous meetings, we agreed to host the national-championship competition at our venue in the middle of summer. Our centre was receiving great reviews and we wanted to ride the wave, thanking Stuart's brother for sending us the boards in the first place and for involving us in a sport we would never on our own have thought to start.

Even though I was busy, nothing could compare with the hours put in by my workhorse husband. Stuart had three separate jobs, filling every hour of the day with work-related activities. He was still acting as outside manager of the tourist farm, which required the normal 40-hour work week. Then he would fill up all his spare time, either helping out at the mountain-boarding centre, or driving off for a weekend to a county fair or showground to perform shows for a fellow Kiwi, for a business called The Sheep Show. And to top it all off, if he could find an evening free he would join the boys down on the slopes, coaching the South-West Mountain-Boarding Team (SWMBT) in preparation for the summer tournament. We did have just one weekend of crazy abandon: we had managed to get tickets for Glastonbury Festival again, and Stuart and I spent the four days there in heaven, dancing together to all the famous artists. The weeks quickly became months. Before I knew it, the time for the national championships had arrived, and we would be hosts to a weekend of spectacular performances.

As one who loved to organise parties, I enjoyed working on the logistics for our event and spent days sorting out the Portaloos, shower units, food trucks and camping area needed for the 500+ spectators and riders that would be descending on us. When the weekend finally arrived the sun shone and everyone on-site was full of cheer, watching the amazing races as the riders gave it their all, pushing themselves to their limits to be the first to pass the finish line. We whooped and cheered as our team members were victorious, beating every other rider in both the downhill and jumping events. With our team shirts firmly in place, we all rejoiced in our achievements. We knew that the event had been a massive success and that our boys would be able to benefit from their newfound fame, going to the highest level in this sport and being invited to compete in the world championships.

I returned home to Vancouver for three weeks after this event and enjoyed showing the photos of our honeymoon to my family and friends. They were captivated by the African photos, and taken aback by the stories that accompanied them. I spent most of this visit with my older sister and my niece, sitting on the beaches of Pasley Island, relaxing in the familiar environment and describing our next planned destination. Mozambique was like another planet to my family; after Googling the country and reading about their recent natural disasters of floods and droughts, combined with the civil unrest in the northern section of this country, they tried to dissuade me from our plans, calling me crazy for wanting to return. It took some convincing, but they eventually accepted my decision, realising that I would go there, with or without their blessing.

And then a glitch came into the plans. My best friend and neighbour, Sarah, was engaged to be married, and they were arranging for the ceremony to take place in Maui, Hawaii. I had grown up having Sarah as my best friend since birth – our mothers were good friends and our fathers were first cousins – and we had always said we'd be each other's maid of honour. She had stood beside me at my wedding and now she was asking me to do the same. The only complication was that I would be halfway across the world at the time. Big problemo. Sarah tried to throw me a lifeline, saying she would totally understand if I couldn't make it. But I promised to start investigating flights that could see me cross the world, from Mozambique to Maui, even though I knew it wasn't going to be a pretty flight plan.

I returned to the UK and settled back into the last few weeks of summer, a signal that we were coming to the end of our six-month work period. We had had a great summer. Even though the months had been very busy with work, we had also made time for fun, attending more music festivals, camping out on the cliffs of Devon with our friends, and joining Marci and Blue's September wedding celebrations. It was an honour for us to be beside our best friends in Devon on their big day, and we all had such a wonderful time watching these two making a life commitment together.

But the ball was rolling and we were preparing for our next six-month adventure, starting with the boys going on a one-month trip to Morocco. Stuart, Tony and Duncan had settled into a rhythm, where each year a different individual chose a destination, sometimes only revealing the climate in order to help with packing, then disclosing the whereabouts at the last minute. This year's trip had been chosen by Tony, the long-haired hippy, who had simply closed his eyes and placed his finger on a rotating globe. He happily announced the northern African country, a place that avoided the dreaded cold climes.

Stuart and I were pleased with our achievements of the last six months and, after a quick trip to Germany to visit his daughter, Marie, we parted ways. Stuart was off on his boys' trip and I was returning to Vancouver, where I would attend several fittings for my bridesmaid's dress. I was prepared to travel solo across the world so that I could make it to Sarah's wedding in January. The month in Vancouver passed quickly; soon I was back on a plane bound for Heathrow airport, where I would meet up with the boys and hear the hilarious accounts of their time in the African country. Since Tony hadn't researched his chosen destination, the boys had been unaware that they would be exploring this Muslim country during the time of Ramadan, the most sacred month of the Islamic calendar. This meant that the locals would fast from first light until sunset, not allowing any food, water or alcohol to touch their lips. Many shops and restaurants are closed at this time out of respect for the custom, and the boys had found it difficult to find food during the day. They had finally gone all out at the end of their trip when they found the only ritzy hotel with a bar open, spending $10 per beer and rejoicing as the liquid touched their parched lips.

And then we were off. New focus: returning to Africa to work off the coast of Mozambique.

This next short section, in italics, is from a journal that I carried everywhere on my travels, but only sporadically made time to update. In fact, you'll see entries only here and in Chapter 13. I could kick myself now and, while I know everyone has different objectives, I would advise anyone who's spending a reasonable amount of time travelling to make a few notes whenever they can. While photos help you to remember places and events, they don't always remind you of the finer details. Reading through the few notes I did make brings back vivid memories of places and people, senses and feelings, things that might otherwise be lost in time.

The one thing that I had forgotten, whether deliberately or not, was the smell of Africa. It didn't take long before it was brought to my senses as we sat on a crowded bus from Mozambique's capital, Maputo, bound for the district of Inhambane. In sharp contrast to the pure beauty of everything that surrounded us, the smell was an acrid, nose-turning scent that made me use my mouth rather than my nose for ventilation. And then there was the bus journey. It started as a struggle, a battle for a seat, a fight for our backpacks to be placed on the same vehicle, a struggle to keep our sanity. And then, after what seemed like a lifetime, we were moving; on our way to a remembered piece of heaven, to the beaches of Inhambane. But not before disaster struck, in the form of car batteries. Sitting behind us on this eight-hour bus journey was a man with several car batteries at his feet. Unfortunately, the batteries weren't properly sealed and some liquid soon became apparent under our seats. At first we thought it was urine, only to discover that it was in fact battery acid. The acid managed to disintegrate my day-pack, my beloved dragon pants and my one and only sweatshirt. Stu's new Aussie hat was also struck, and the forest-green colouration was quickly replaced by a yellow, puckish appearance. And the fun didn't stop there ... the bus broke down, coming to a loud, grinding halt beside a small Mozambican village, causing a stiflingly hot, two-hour delay to our journey.

When we finally arrived at our end destination, back at the Bamboozi resort at the far end of the small coastal village of Tofo, we were unclear about the roles we would take on. Des, the owner of the resort, was away in South Africa, and Stuart had to fight our case over the next two weeks, getting involved in more than one heavy discussion. The management of the dive centre of the resort had changed hands, and the new managers didn't want to honour the job positions that we had been offered the year before. We had been promised to get certified as dive masters (DM) on an intensive scuba programme, where we would need to put in hundreds of hours both in and out of the water. We would need to pass successfully through different levels of training, in exchange for working in the dive centre and resort bar. Finally, Stuart managed to secure our positions working in the dive centre, where we were each allocated an instructor to help us achieve our dive-master status.

Unfortunately, my instructor was a jerk. Having only recently acquired his own instructor's qualification, he thought he was superior in some way and smugly informed me that he didn't think I would be able to achieve the DM level in the available time frame. He was condescending and gave so little of himself that it pushed me harder to excel in all the different areas of the program. I quickly worked through the book work and tests of the first two levels: Open Water Diver and Advanced Open Water Diver. Stuart also pushed through the assignments, advancing at a quicker pace as he had more underwater experience than I did, and we both put in long hours in order to achieve our goal.

Now, I'd be lying if I said all we did was work – I have never partied as hard as we did in those few months. We formed an international posse, individuals from all over the globe converging together on Mozambican soil to work in one of the dive centres, with the common interest of blowing bubbles under water and partying hard. It wasn't uncommon to see us all partying until the early hours of the morning, dancing on the tables of Fatima's Bar, holding on to one another in laughter and merriment. Night after night we joined each other for dinner or drinks, strengthening the bonds of friendship that would last a lifetime.

And then it was time for me to go; destination: Maui. We had made arrangements for me to travel to South Africa with three fellow Aussie backpackers to Nelspruit Backpackers, before taking the

The Way of the Explorer

shuttle to Jo'burg International airport. Stuart was extremely nervous as I left him, not liking the idea of a single, blue-eyed blonde on her own in one of the most dangerous cities in the world, but he knew that I had my mind set. So, with a final hug and kiss, Stuart and I parted ways and I set off on my epic journey. Step 1: overland from Mozambique to South Africa. Step 2: flight from South Africa to London. Step 3: flight from London to Los Angeles. Step 4: flight from LA to Honolulu, Hawaii; overnight with my older sister's friend. Step 5: flight from Honolulu to Maui, Hawaii.

At last, having travelled halfway across the world, my new focus would be the wedding. The next two-and-a-half weeks passed quickly, and I had great times with my best friend, cousins, older sister and brother-in-law as we all celebrated Christmas, New Year and wedding functions together.

After the ceremony I returned with Weeze and her husband, Rob, to the island of Oahu, where we spent a few days on our own, enjoying the sunny days and warm ocean waters. We all took lessons in surfing and became tourists, visiting the famous North Shore. And then my time was up. My flight plan reversed, I spent the next two days in travel, crossing the world to return to my husband and to continue with my qualifications in the diving world.

I had been back at Bamboozi for less than 48 hours when it happened. Someone died ... an underwater freediver. Stuart knew the individual, a 24-year-old Aussie named Brad, whom he had picked up from the Inhambane bus station and brought back to our resort. Police and representatives from the Australian consulate were present to go through the formalities of the death certificate and to repatriate the body from foreign soils. The vibe in the air changed as we all tried to rationalise what had happened. My heart went out to my co-workers, those who had had to go back down under the sea to search for and retrieve the cold and stiff body from its clutches, and then sit beside the corpse as they headed back to shore, a 25-minute journey. It would take several weeks before this scene could be laid to rest, and our lesson would be the seriousness of this underwater sport and just how careful we needed to be to stay safe.

Our diving was becoming more and more extreme; the currents off the Mozambican coast were intense, easily sweeping a diver hundreds of metres away within minutes. We were forced to do negative entries, where as soon as we rolled back into the water from the side of the boat, we swam as hard as we could to the bottom, grabbing on to one of the outcrops of rock to keep ourselves from being swept away. This type of diving was not for the fainthearted and we were pushed to our limits, slowing our breath to try to get the most time possible under water, while at the same time supervising our clients, some of whom refused to accept the dangers of those waters. We went on exploration dives, dropping into sites that had never been probed and visiting famous dive spots to interact with a huge variety of sea creatures.

One of the best sites was Manta Reef. We would descend to about 90 feet and then wait beside the cleaning station, where manta rays hover while 'cleaner fish' remove external parasites from their bodies. Here we watched, enchanted as the massive, black manta rays soared towards us with their wing-like movements. They settled inches above us, hovering as the bubbles from our tanks washed over their ventral surface, obviously producing a nice sensation for them.

The manta ray is one of the largest in the world, with a wingspan of up to 20 feet; and as you peer from underneath a ray, so close that you could touch it, you know you are experiencing something truly unique.

Mantas were not the only large fish we swam with. This area is known for its whale sharks, and we were fortunate to see dozens of these creatures, once spotting 18 of them on a single trip out to a dive site. These slow-moving, filter-feeding sharks are the largest known fish species, reaching lengths of up to 40 feet. We often viewed them from below on a dive as they swam at the surface and blocked out rays of sunlight, and we sometimes snorkelled with them after we spotted them from the dive boat. We were cautious never to touch the majestic animals as they have a layer of mucus to protect them against infection; sometimes we had to swim backstroke to get out of their way as they approached us.

On one occasion, after spending a good 45 minutes snorkelling with one of these giants, we reboarded the boat and sat stunned as the animal lifted its head out of the water and proceeded to rest it on the side of our inflatable vessel. We enjoyed the amazing sight, spending several minutes just gazing at this wonderful sea creature, loving the trust that it showed us and knowing we were experiencing an extremely rare and special moment.

The days were filled with sunshine and intense heat. The white sand on the dunes and around the dive shop became so hot that we had to sprint across an area; every grain of sand that touched our feet felt like a hot iron, and walking barefoot was asking for trouble. Our tans were deepening and we were becoming fit and healthy from lugging the heavy scuba tanks around, from vehicle to boat and back again – our customers were not expected to carry anything apart from their snorkels, masks and fins.

The days here were predictable and flowed from one to the next, and it was one of the guests that gave us forewarning of a big change that was about to happen. The strongest recorded tropical cyclone was on its way south. Having devastated Madagascar with its high winds, storm surge and flooding rains, it was now making its way to us via the Mozambique Channel. Equalling a category-five hurricane in the North Atlantic, this massive cyclone was catastrophic, and reports started to filter in about the increasing levels of deaths, injuries and homelessness due to this natural disaster. I had never experienced anything like this, and helped in rapidly shutting down and barricading the dive shop and restaurant.

When the tropical storm front – a by-product of the massive cyclone – hit us, I ran to my tent for cover. Stuart had positioned our tent inside the bush line that separated the coconut grove from the sand dune and the sea, and figured we were in a safer position there than exposed to the elements. We noticed as the storm increased in intensity and watched in amazement as the coconut trees were forced onto their sides, almost parallel to the ground. Coconuts were ripped from their branches, hurled about in the wind as if they were weightless. Branches and other debris were flying through the air, and I thanked Stuart for having the foresight to put our tent in a position where we were protected from the elements. The only thing that could reach us was the wind and, as we lay watching from our tent, we could feel its breath as the top roof of our tent pushed down onto our bodies, making us feel like sardines squished in a can.

Nature finally calmed down and we were able to resume our daily lives, although we had to halt our diving for a week due to the aftermath of the storm – the incredibly rough seas were not worth the risk.

While on dry land I continued with my studies, working my way through the Rescue Diver course and finally beginning my divemaster certification. I now had to train both my mind and my body, having to undertake nine written examinations as well as the five physical tests. Stuart accompanied me on my swimming test, where my instructor drove us out past the breaking surf and to a point an estimated mile out from shore. I then had to swim to the beach as fast as I could, having to make it within a certain time limit. Unfortunately, the waters were filled with bluebottle jellyfish, small invertebrates with venomous tentacles that deliver a painful sting. With tears in my eyes, feeling the painful tentacles strike my skin, I forced myself to go on and not to abort the swim; I knew that my instructor would not give me another chance to make it up. Stuart yelled encouragement from the boat as it followed my course, unaware that I was being stung by jellyfish, then finally jumped into the waters himself, wanting to help me out once I had reached the shores. He was shocked when he saw the state I was in and ran to the only restaurant on the sand dunes, returning with a bottle of vinegar and pouring the solution over top of the welts that were developing, in the hope of neutralising the stings. But the pain was worth it: I had completed the swim within the required time. Even though I looked like I had been whipped, with major welts that would stay with me for a week appearing across my cheeks, neck, arms, legs and back, I smiled on the inside. I knew that I was almost there, at the end of my training to become a dive master.

We were moving up in the world; Bamboozi's owner, Des, was leaving for a month and asked if Stuart and I would like to house-sit for him. This meant we could say goodbye to our very sandy and overheated tent, and hello to a home with a proper bed, fans, bathroom and kitchen. We jumped at the opportunity and it wasn't long before we relaxed in our new accommodation, buying crayfish, brought to our door by the local fishermen, for a dollar each. We loved our time here, so much so that we started looking into real estate in the area, and found a square mile of beachfront for sale for only £3,000! We were very tempted but, after much deliberation, felt the purchase would be too large a commitment; it would force us to return exclusively to this country when we still had many places on the planet that we wanted to explore.

The end was in sight and, having finally completed our DM course, we were each given a separate 'graduation ceremony'. Not to be found in the official books of the Padi Dive Master Program, the evening celebration was organised by the dive-centre staff, and involved the infamous 'funnel'. A two-litre plastic Coke bottle with the bottom cut off is inverted and filled with an assortment of local spirits. The graduate then has to take a deep breath and drink the entire concoction, downing over 15 ounces of hard liquor in one go. After my turn, my fellow divers patted me on the back – I was one of the only girls not to run to the bathroom and chuck it all up. We then spent the rest of the night dancing on the tables, loving our time with our close group of friends, while painfully aware that we would soon be leaving this special place.

We had so many great memories of our time in Tofo and we were sad when it was time for us to leave. Just a few days after becoming dive masters, we packed our backpacks and made our way north to the coastal town of Vilanculos, where we had organised a week's tour to some of the nearby islands. It was great to be back in the role of guest rather than worker, and we enjoyed being shown the sights of the area, sailing across the waters on the local dhows and loving the culinary delights that were served to us.

The days passed quickly and we were soon back on a bus, heading to the capital, Maputo, and then across the border, returning to stay at Nelspruit Backpackers in South Africa. We rented a car for our last two weeks and revisited Kruger National Park, as well as travelling to a new country: Swaziland.

Known to be one of the smallest countries in Africa, Swaziland is no more than 200 kilometres from north to south, and 130 kilometres east to west. It is a country within a country, encircled mainly by South Africa and sharing only a small, north-eastern border with Mozambique. We entered the country in search of the wild animals, knowing that this was a place with a very diverse topography and varying climate, with the cool, mountainous high region and its hot and dry low region.

We headed to the Mlilwane Wildlife Sanctuary, Swaziland's pioneer conservation area – a beautiful, secluded sanctuary situated in the kingdom's Ezulwini Valley, the 'Valley of Heavens'. Here we spent days following the network of self-guided trails, traversing on foot through a variety of habitats, strolling leisurely past wildebeest, zebras, kudus, impalas and warthogs. We would then return, carefree and relaxed, to the sanctuary's Sondzela Backpackers hostel and get changed for the pool. From there we watched in stunned disbelief as the resident ostriches tried to lay claim to our belongings, and we laughed as we watched a fellow backpacker try unsuccessfully to stand up to this bird, the largest and heaviest living bird on the planet. He quickly admitted defeat and ran from the scene, after receiving several painful jabs from the bird's beak.

Our time was nearing its end and, with more of the sanctuary to explore, we decided to hire a local Swazi guide. We knew that the area was partitioned into different areas, with different game animals separated from one another for their own protection. We would need someone to open and close the gates of these different sections, as well as informing us about which animals we should look out for. Our vehicle also now held a fourth passenger, an Irish girl called Shelley, whom we had befriended at the hostel.

We toured around on the different dirt roads, watching and photographing the African wildlife from the comfort of our cushioned seats and quizzing our guide on the specifics of the park. At one point we were surrounded by four young lions, all looking inside our car. Knowing that our insurance wouldn't cover damage brought on by animal encounters, we prayed that the lions wouldn't jump up and damage the vehicle. After leaving this section of the park we drove along the roads, our guide now telling us to be on the lookout for rhinos. It wasn't long before we spotted two of them, a mother and her calf about a kilometre away, hidden among a few trees on the far side of a watering hole. Our guide told Stuart to park the car and for us all to get out, and we all followed his lead as he started to walk in the direction of the rhinos, skirting the watering hole and coming to stand behind one of the trees. Stuart questioned him about our proximity to these wild animals but, after receiving many assurances about our safety, Stu equated our experience to visiting a zoo, where the animals were tame and used to human contact. Our Swazi leader continued to motion us forward, away from our hiding spots behind the trees, in order to take closer-range photographs of the two animals. It was as we posed for these pictures, only metres away from the massive beasts, that the scene suddenly changed.

The mother rhino, which had been absent-mindedly chomping on the grass, swiftly lifted her head and turned in our direction, sniffing the air to determine her surroundings. Her well-developed sense of smell was far superior to her poor eyesight in revealing the landscape, and this is when she became aware of our presence. We soon realised that we were in a very dangerous position. We had been led way too close to a mother and her offspring, a scenario that I remembered Stuart always saying was one of the most treacherous scenes: a mother is always highly protective of her young and will act aggressively to defend it in any way. With this in mind, we started to move back very cautiously, making no sudden movements that might spook the animal, all the while hearing our guide say, 'Walk, don't run. If you run, she will charge you. Walk, walk, walk faster!' He kept repeating it, 'Walk, walk. No, walk faster, faster. No, no – don't run!', gesturing with his hands as we backed away, cautioning us not to make a speedy getaway.

Stuart had been watching the body language of the mother and, as he saw the signs that showed her agitation change to aggression, we followed his command to 'RUN!!!!' I have never sprinted so hard in all my life and, when I quickly scanned to my side, I could see my other three companions legging it as well, trying to put as much distance between us and this charging animal. At one point, I thought to veer off to the side, thinking I might be safer to go around the watering hole on the opposite side to everyone else, but thankfully changed my mind and continued headlong towards the car, finally arriving at the vehicle and leaping into the back seat in one piece. The four doors closed as we all sealed ourselves in. Just a couple of seconds later we could see the mother rhino pause just a few metres from our car, smelling the air to track down our scent, then finally giving up on us and returning to her calf, which had followed the chase from behind. After we regained our breath, we sat motionless for several minutes, shocked by our near-fatal encounter, knowing that we would have been a goner if the mother had reached us. There is no doubt we could have been crushed to death by this 4,000 lb beast.

Thankful to be alive, we returned home to recount our story to our fellow backpackers and cheered Shelley's 30th birthday as well as our day's adventures, drinking long into the night. Our African expedition was at an end and, with great memories and our dive-master certification, we left the hot continent, returning to the rainy and cold climes of the south-west of England. We were blissfully unaware that a major change was on its way.

Chapter 10
Where to Now?

'I'm done.' I had heard Stuart say this numerous times, ever since I had first arrived on the scene four years earlier, but this time I knew he meant it. He had worked at the same tourist farm in England for the past decade and now needed a change, to find a new path that would lead to more opportunities and a greater amount of savings. We started to look out for different jobs, broadening our search to include New Zealand and Canada, never knowing what lay ahead but being open to anything.

At the same time, I was extremely busy at the mountain-boarding centre, increasing the number of staff to accommodate the large groups arriving at our tracks. We were now endeavouring to make our business as sellable as possible, knowing that we would be leaving at the end of the season and not coming back. Stuart went to meetings all over the county trying to find someone to take on our extreme-sport centre and, with only weeks left in the country, we had our first nibble. One of our local boys, Sam, who enjoyed the sport himself and had helped as an instructor at the centre, wanted to take the business on but wasn't sure if he could find the funds. We were asking for £10,000 – a reasonable price, considering that the centre was well established as well as being lined up to host the World Championships the following year.

As we approached the end of the season, a decision had to be made. Job offers were coming in and we now had three options: 1) stay in

Devon, with the offer of an increase in wages for managing the tourist farm and running the mountain-boarding centre; 2) move to the east of the UK, with Stuart working full-time for the six-month season for the Sheep Show (which he was already engaged in most weekends); or 3) move to the North Island of New Zealand, where Stuart could become manager of a tourist farm, called Sheep World. The latter would be a massive commitment, requiring the standard 12 months of work every year with just 3 weeks of holiday.

After much deliberation, comparing the pros and cons of each position, we decided to go for the job in the county of Norfolk, with Stuart taking on the demonstrator position for the Sheep Show. This was a wonderful family business, and the job would allow us to continue our lifestyle of six months of work followed by six months of travel.

In the last weeks of summer, Stuart started an intensive driving program, spending hours studying for his LGV (large goods vehicle) qualifications. He used up any spare time out on the roads with an instructor, trying to get comfortable behind the wheel of these large trucks. He met with both successes and failures, but misfortune stood in his path: when he went for his final driving test the passenger seat belt failed and the test had to be aborted. He was unable to accept the new test date as we would be out of the country by that date, so Stuart held a weight on his shoulders as we prepared to leave England. He knew that he still had a mountain to climb when we returned from our six months away, when he would have to complete his LGV driving test, as well as passing his 'artic' (articulated vehicle) qualifications, one of the toughest levels to master in the driving world.

Where to Now?

When it was time to say goodbye once and for all to the beautiful county of Devon, I had tears in my eyes and a heavy heart. We had such an amazing circle of friends here – our workmates, neighbours and all the mountain-boarding team – that I was really going to miss this setting. But above all, I felt sad that we would no longer be in close proximity to Marci and Blue, Adel and Tony. They were special souls who had attended our wedding and the epic Glastonbury festival, and had made our time in Devon so special.

It was in the final 48 hours before our departure that we received great news: the money had been found to buy our mountain-boarding centre; we were overjoyed when the cheque cleared and we were £10,000 richer. Our life possessions were stuffed into our car and, with a final farewell, we drove to the county of Norfolk in the east, where our new home would be. After placing all of our belongings into storage on the new boss's farm, we headed to London, where we had plans to meet up with Tony and Adel before flying off on our six-month adventure.

Even though I had lived in the UK for four years, I had never experienced the London nightlife, and nothing could have prepared me for what lay ahead. Adel's older sister had visited us when we were in Devon, bringing her friend with her, and Stuart had helped the girls as they tried to learn the intricacies of horseback riding, spending hours tutoring her friend, helping her gain her confidence as she rode around the farm. Now we were on their home turf. Both girls worked for a famous high-class gentlemen's club that was managed by the friend's fiancé, and they wanted to thank us for their holiday in Devon and treat us to dinner. After dressing up, we set off for our night's adventures, taking the Tube to arrive at the high-end strip club, where we would be treated to VIP service and great food.

I had been to sex clubs before – it's almost a touristy thing to do when in Amsterdam or in Thailand – so wasn't shocked to be brought to this establishment of topless women, and I enjoyed the special treatment we received as we were guided to a table in the VIP section. We were given a selection of drinks and each of us received a token for a private dancer. Stuart laughed as I was led away for my private dance (only slightly perturbed that I didn't give him my token), knowing what lay ahead. My dancing girl was beautiful and, as she gyrated on my lap, with her breasts jiggling in front of me, I laughed at the hilariousness of the situation and tried to enjoy the moment. The music was pumping through the establishment and we all enjoyed the night's activities, dancing, drinking, eating and over-indulging our senses. We continued to party until the early hours of the morning, when we finally had to pull ourselves away in order to go to the airport in time for our flight.

We must have looked quite a sight as we dragged ourselves into Heathrow airport, our energy from the night's activities dissipating, struggling to keep our eyes open and to get ourselves checked in. I fell asleep as soon as we boarded our plane, and didn't wake up until we touched down in Los Angeles, a stopover on our way to Vancouver. We must have drawn up a red flag at Heathrow – as we exited the plane in LA, Stuart was stopped by a policeman with a sniffer dog. They had been waiting in the plane's gangway, an area I'd never seen police in before. As Stuart started to walk past, the dog immediately affixed itself to Stuart's trousers, preventing him from walking forward, and then sniffed at his crotch. Stuart smiled and said that the dog had a great sense of smell, detecting the scent of his bitch (female dog) that had been in season before he left, trying to give a reason for the canine's interest. The policeman smiled and responded in an over-friendly manner, saying, 'You know what type of dog this is, don't you? He's a drug dog and you've obviously got something on you, so it would be easier for you if you just came clean now and showed me what you've got.' We were certainly not carrying drugs on us and, as Stuart was pulled out of the line to stand at the side of the gangway, I continued on my path, knowing that Stuart could hold his own and that I needn't be involved.

It was 15 minutes before I saw Stuart walking towards me, and he was stopped on another two occasions as we made our way to our gate. When we finally did board our final plane, we ordered a stiff drink and smiled at all that had transpired in the last 24 hours, laughing as scenes of the night before surfaced in our memories.

Our time in Vancouver passed as a blur, kept busy with the newest arrival to our family: my little niece, Sofia. I was with my sister and her husband in the hospital room, watching as Weeze endured 24 hours of labour, before the doctors suddenly pulled her into the birthing room for an emergency caesarean when the baby's heart rate started to drop. The whole experience was quite traumatising and it backed up our decision not have children of our own, giving us further ammunition when people asked us our plans in terms of progeny.

I was also scheduled to spend a week of learning – my mum had enrolled me onto an intensive course at the university, called Remote Viewing. This was a new area of exploration for me; I had taken other courses and studies in the metaphysical world, some that involved healing like Reiki and Seichem, and others that involved the explanation of other dimensions and the angelic realm. This new method had been sponsored and developed in the early 1970s by the US government and had its roots in quantum science. The Department of Defence defined it as 'The learned ability to transcend space and time, to view persons, places or things remote in space and time; to gather and report information on the same.' In its early development the researchers had brought together known psychics and telepaths, individuals such as Uri Geller, with heightened extra-sensory perception, and after years of intense study discovered the methodology on how those people received and analysed the information. Remote Viewing practice had been developed at the time of the Cold War, with the intention of spying on the real or perceived enemies of the US nation, and was a classified program within the CIA for over two decades.

Following the declassification of documents relating to this program in the 1990s, one of its former members, David Morehouse, was teaching the public this methodology, and now I was going to learn it. Morehouse made the subject real for me by equating it all to science. In the world of quantum physics everything is energy and energy is everything; therefore, on some level, everything can be expressed in waveform. It is this waveform expression of the target and all of its components that the viewer perceives and then records, in the form of visual and verbal data. This week of learning reinforced how special we humans are. It has taken innumerable events to get us to the point where we are today, billions of years of manifestation, and it is this energy, used to create everything, that is also inside us. We are given the power to create and to connect with this timeless energy in every moment. This is a powerful tool and I am grateful to be aware of it. And so, after six full days of sessions, I was a firm believer in Remote Viewing, with a new respect for the universe, its energy and our connection to it all.

When the time came for us to depart Vancouver, I packed our bags with tears in my eyes. No matter how many times I leave my family, the farewells are always difficult, and I often find myself trying to regain my composure as I walk up to the ticket counter. But I soon regained my optimism as we made our way across the Pacific, heading for the North Island of New Zealand, where Stuart's brother Craig had taken on the manager's role at the tourist farm called Sheep World. Over the next few weeks, Stuart and I watched as Craig and his wife, Vicki, made a healthy profit by buying, doing up and selling a house and, following their lead, bought ourselves a four-bedroom property in the same area, financed with money from the sale of the mountain-boarding centre. With an exchange rate of 1 to 2.5, our money was able to stretch a lot further than normal, and we rejoiced in our new role as property owners, quickly filling the house with tenants.

We then flew to the South Island to stay with Stuart's older sister, Louise, and it was here where we celebrated Christmas, before learning of the devastating news of the December 26th tsunami. We all sat in front of the television, watching as one of the deadliest natural disasters in recorded history shook the world. Then our shock soon turned to worry as we realised that our best mates, Tony and Adel, were on the island closest to the earthquake's epicentre. We spent the next 48 hours filled with fear, tormented by the scenes of death and destruction that filled our screens, and praying for the safety of our friends. The death toll continued to increase in staggering numbers, moving quickly from the tens of thousands to over two hundred thousand; we couldn't believe the extent of damage as the tsunami's waves hit shores across the globe. We were relieved when we received an email from our friends, briefly describing their flight for survival, including their walk to safety, where they had had to step over the dead bodies in their path to get out of the area. My heart went out to all the families that were affected by this carnage, and a black cloud surrounded us all over this Christmas period. Celebrations were officially over.

After leaving New Zealand, we made our way to Malaysia, where Stuart and I would travel by bus and boat to reach the eastern Perhentian Islands. The relaxed atmosphere of the waterfront chalets, combined with the white sands, crystal-clear waters and great diving, gave us time to refocus on the present and allowed the memories of the devastation of the tsunami to filter to the backs of our minds. We felt blessed to be alive, to have each other and to know that our best friends were safely out of harm's way.

After a few weeks on one of the beautiful islands, it was time for Stuart and me to go on our individual travels. Stuart was headed for the Philippines for the month-long boys' trip, on which they would be joined by a fourth member, a friend from Devon called Tim. I would meanwhile return home to Canada for some more family time. As always, our time apart flew by, and before we knew it, we were back in each other's arms in Kuala Lumpur, with the only change being the new 'Om' symbol tattooed on Stuart's chest. All the boys had had this tattoo inked while they were in the Philippines, and I was shocked to hear of Duncan's plight after the procedure: he had cut off the circulation to his arm while holding it still against a plastic chair during the painful procedure, and it was a few months before he regained the use of his hand.

As Stuart and I walked along the streets of the capital of Malaysia, we discovered that we were present at the time of Thaipusam, one of the Hindu community's yearly festivals. We made our way to one of the most popular Hindu shrines outside of India, the famous Batu Caves. We climbed the 272 steps to reach the entrance to the caves, moving forward at an incredibly slow pace amongst a crowd of thousands, and were astounded as the limestone hill transformed itself into a series of smaller internal caves, decorated by Hindu paintings, statues and shrines. But what really took my breath away was witnessing the kavadi bearers, Hindu devotees dressed in traditional clothing and carrying bowed wooden or metal-framed structures upon their shoulders, some of which rose up to two metres. The frames held long skewers, at the end of which were sharpened hooks that pierced the skin of the bearers' torsos. I watched as one of the bearers, who had clearly just made the arduous climb, sat down close to me, and I couldn't believe the number of hooks that pierced his body. I could tell by his rolling eyes that he was in some kind of trance and I backed away as one of the priests neared, holding a smoking container of consecrated ash, which he started to sprinkle over the pierced flesh.

After a week in the capital we flew to Borneo, a new location for both of us where we enjoyed amazing encounters with the native wildlife both in and out of the water. We spent our first week in the native bush, arranging to stay at 'Uncle Tan's Camp', a location set deep within the tropical rain forest. We were ferried by speedboat to the camp, a two-hour journey up river, and I started to get excited as we passed lush foliage and several species of monkeys. It felt like we were seeing nature as it was meant to be seen, untouched by man. After settling into our accommodation – a raised hut with no doors or windows and with only a light mattress with a mosquito net – we met our local guide, ready to go on a guided trek into the surrounding jungle area. These walking safaris would set out either first thing in the morning or late at night, guiding us into the remote native bush, and we stayed close together as we had been warned how easy it was to get lost in the depths of the jungle. Our guide's knowledge of the fauna and flora was astounding, and he pointed out creatures that were expertly camouflaged, introducing us to animals we'd never seen before. He even taught us how to spot spiders in the pitch dark of night, positioning our flashlights at a certain angle whereby we could decipher their whereabouts due to the beam of light reflecting from their tiny eyes.

Our days here were packed with wildlife viewings as we embarked on a number of river safaris, cruising down the river waters and often stopping to take shots of the vast numbers of bird species, crocodiles, turtles and river otters. We came close to the endangered proboscis monkey, an endemic primate with a distinctly unique face. But our main goal was to see the elusive orangutan. We extended our time here to find more of these extraordinary mammals, which share 96 per cent of their DNA with humans, and are on the endangered list due to the destruction of their natural habitat. We were ecstatic when we finally found two up a tree, but quickly had to give them some distance when they started to throw branches down at us. The orangutans were not as overjoyed as we were by our encounter.

After this time in the jungle, we made our way to the south of Borneo, landing a four-week stint working for a dive centre in the coastal town of Semporna, allowing us to dive at some of the best dive spots in the world. The boat trips headed to the world-famous islands of Sipadan and Mabul, home to thousands of turtles, schooling sharks, swirling barracuda and to the awe-inspiring coral walls, which drop more than 2,000 metres straight down to the sea floor. The islands have the world's most diverse marine ecosystem, and we could give clients a money-back guarantee that dives would include turtles and sharks. Divers had to be very careful not to be swept away by the strong currents, and I was immensely grateful for my intensive training in the extreme conditions of the Mozambican waters.

My experience was to be tested: I once had to rescue one of my divers, who was panicking frantically 30 feet underwater as she was unable to ascend due to a reverse ear block. Sending the rest of the group up with Stuart, I took her into the depths before slowly making an ascent when I could see that the trapped air had dissipated, allowing her to move up through the column of water without pain. We had very little air left in our tanks in those extra minutes underwater and we had to remain calm as the strong currents knocked us off balance, holding each other's arms to keep us together. Stuart recognised the seriousness of this situation and returned underwater with a spare tank of air; however, we were able to surface with just enough air.

Our dives at this location were truly amazing. One of the most memorable was when we were encircled by thousands of barracuda, each on average between four and five feet in length, watching as they swam around us with their mouths open, exposing their needle-like teeth, all the while with six large sharks positioned on the sea floor below us. When I noticed some of the barracuda training their eyes on me, I quickly hid the metallic knife that I used to tap on my tank to get my guests' attention underwater; I didn't want to appear as if I was holding a small fish and then myself end up as the barracudas' main course. The wildlife was astounding; dive after dive we encountered new species, hidden within the crevices of the rocks or swimming up to us from the depths.

Before leaving Borneo we visited the Sepilok Orangutan Rehabilitation Centre, a wonderful establishment that takes in orphaned, hurt or rescued orangutans from around the countryside. This creature's natural habitat was being destroyed as palm-oil plantations were taking over the landscape, and we learned of the dwindling numbers of this amazing mammal, causing it to be listed on the endangered-species list.

We were delighted to view orangutans in close proximity, and watched as they made their way from the depths of the forest, grabbing on to the ropes secured between a network of trees. Hand over hand, they made their way to the feeding platforms and ate the fruit on offer, their mannerisms so closely resembling those of humans that it really hit home how similar they are to us.

After some time we went for a walk with a ranger on one of the designated tracks and watched as the leeches tried to get a free ride and meal, extending their hook-like mouths towards us as we brushed past the bushes they were in. We were on the lookout for some of the older orangutans, those that had been at the centre for a while. They had been released into a large enclosure, several acres in size, and we craned our heads up in the hope of spotting one in the foliage above us. Unfortunately, with our focus on the trees above, Stuart did not see the giant centipede that had wedged itself within the tree stump built into the viewing platform. When he decided to sit down for a rest on the tree stump, he received the most painful bite of his life. I was shocked when he leapt into the air, his profane language relaying the severe pain burning at the top, inside region of his leg. My concern grew as the ranger became anxious as we watched the foot-long insect retreat into the bush. Our guide immediately called his headquarters and was informed that we would need to get to a hospital as soon as we returned to the base. We struggled to help Stuart, who was almost doubled over in pain, make the long trek back through the bush. My husband is a tough cookie, very rarely showing any signs of pain, but the symptoms from the venomous bite were coming on strong. As soon as we arrived back at the headquarters we were again urged to go immediately to the hospital. But my husband is not a fan of hospitals. When a fellow backpacker heard of our ordeal and offered Stuart his penicillin, the drug that we knew would be administered by the hospital doctors, he accepted, determined now to return to our accommodation. I became his nurse that night, trying as best as I could to help with the headache, nausea, itching and painful swelling, a little frightened when his man parts swelled to an unimaginable size. Stuart had received numerous bites and stings over his lifetime but this one topped them all, and it scared me to see the love of my life in such severe pain. Thankfully, within 24 hours the pain and swelling had receded, and the only evidence of the encounter were the two small puncture wounds in his upper leg.

Before leaving Borneo we visited a sanctuary that looked after the endemic proboscis monkey. We were fascinated by this reddish-brown monkey, with its distinctive feature of a very large, bulbous nose. We walked through the grounds, carefully picking our way through thousands of crabs on the muddy floors of the mangrove forest, and listening to the various vocalisations of the monkeys in the distance, laughing at the calls that sounded like honks from a sick car.

We returned to the mainland of Malaysia for our last two weeks, transporting ourselves by bus and boat to Tioman Island, a beautiful haven in the South China Sea. It was here that we met up with Tony and Adel and heard the details of the tsunami, listening to the heart-wrenching story of their flight for survival and lamenting the scenes of tragedy that still affected so many individuals. We focused then on the present, enjoying each other's company like never before. We knew that we would soon all be returning to the UK, but for the first time to different locations.

And then our time was up. After our boat ride to the mainland we headed south to Singapore, where we would be boarding our return flight to England. Another six months had come and gone, filled with both wonderful and harrowing tales. Now it was time to return to work, in a new and undiscovered location. Norfolk, here we come!

Chapter 11
Turkey Plucking and Honduras

Everything was flat. The England I knew comprised rolling hillsides, but things were different here in Norfolk. The horizon seemed to stretch as far as the eye could see and the land lay low, seeming to stretch out for ever in a horizontal plane.

We had moved into a small brick cottage on a farm close to the farm that belonged to Stuart's boss. This was our first accommodation where we could walk around in the nude (if we so desired) – there was no one to walk in on us unexpectedly, and no other roommates to invade our space. Stuart would work a normal five-day week – a novelty, since he was used to working for more than one employer at a time – and I would re-enter the workforce, signing on with a temping agency to work as a supply/substitute teacher.

Teaching in Devon had never been a possibility as the schools were spread out around the county and there had been a surplus of teachers desperate for the positions available. But within a week of being in Norfolk, I was teaching in a nearby school. At first I was quite nervous, having been out of the loop for a good four years and never having taught in England, but it didn't take long for me to regain my confidence. Kids are kids, no matter where you are in the world. The fact that I had a foreign accent and a dream lifestyle immediately caught the students' attention, and I would entice them with stories of our global travels, entertaining them with my tales once they had finished the schoolwork that had been set.

I was often called back to work at the schools in my area as I was a far cry from the typical supply teacher; the headteachers seemed to be impressed by my energy and enthusiasm and my experience of travelling the world. I was competent at teaching the material set, and I also broadened the students' minds in terms of the infinite possibilities available to them if they just thought outside the box. I encouraged them all to take a gap year before university, to take themselves away from the security and stability of home, to stand on their own two feet and venture to see the world and all that it has to offer. I corrected their inexperienced concepts of needing thousands of pounds to travel, assuring them that it was inexpensive to travel in third-world countries, such as those I had explored in Southeast Asia.

Students often sought me out at lunchtime to chat, leaving with smiles on their faces and, hopefully, new dreams in their hearts. Over the next few months dozens of students told me how I had changed their perceptions of the world and that they were now excited about their future. Brilliant!

Another exciting prospect was becoming a godmother for the first time. My best friend, Sarah, gave birth to a healthy baby girl whom she named Pasley, and asked me to be her godmother. Having a very special connection with my own godmother, I was overjoyed to be asked to have this relationship with my best friend's daughter, and looked forward to meeting the little angel when I returned to Vancouver in the summer.

I was also looking forward to seeing my parents' new home; they had sold their house in Vancouver and bought a place on Bowen Island, their dream retirement destination. It was a place that was familiar to us as we always crossed the island in order to get to Bowen Bay, a private marina where we stored our boat in order to get to our summer cabin on Pasley Island. In fact, our summer cabin in North Bay was in full view from the front deck of their new place and, being 300 metres above sea level, they enjoyed amazing vistas of the many islands in the area, with views of the snow-capped mountains in the distance. The Howe Sound area was stunningly beautiful, with the distance sounds of the waves crashing on the shores below, and it was common for bald eagles to fly at eye level past their windows, soaring above the treetops.

I was very grateful to my parents. Year after year, they helped cover most of the cost of my plane tickets to allow me to return to Canada in the summer months to reconnect with my family and friends. I packed as much as I could into my three-week stay there this year, spending time with my parents, sisters, nieces and cousins, and meeting my goddaughter for the first time. I had a great time and felt very close to my two best friends, Sarah and Amber. I also made time to complete my next level in Remote Viewing, broadening my understanding and my techniques in the methodology on another six-day intensive course, gaining a heightened respect for energy and how we can tune in to it.

When I returned to England I joined Stuart at a couple of his shows, watching as he captivated audiences with his New Zealand charm and wacky sense of humour, and felt very proud when the crowds roared with delight. My man was very good at what he did and it didn't surprise me when audience members sought his counsel, asking for help with their horses or dogs.

By the time our season of work came to an end we realised we were in a difficult situation: we had no money to travel and would therefore not be going on our six-month holiday. DAMMIT! Stuart did not like to be in debt and the New Zealand mortgage hung around his neck like a heavy chain, so every cent we had made over the summer was being sent overseas with the goal of paying off our mortgage within five years. We were broke, and I gratefully accepted a teaching position, even though the subject was not my speciality – ICT (computer studies) had completely changed since my days in school. I had taught at the school before, and the principal believed that if you were a good teacher you could teach any subject, so hired me as the ICT teacher, employing an ICT expert to work as my full-time assistant.

In the meantime, Stuart picked up work driving sugar-beet trucks. This was a very dangerous job as he had to drive massive, heavily weighed-down trucks along country lanes, only narrowly escaping collisions as cars whipped around the blind corners. After a few months he happily handed in his notice, only to land a job at a turkey-plucking factory – we were desperate for the money and it was the only job on offer. When my school contract ended I tried to make extra cash working alongside Stuart, but stuck it out for only three hours; I would dry-heave behind the mask that covered my nose and mouth, detesting my job of pulling out the broken feather quills. Get me out of here!

Luckily, Stuart's best friend, Tony, offered us a lifeline, knowing that we were not enjoying our first winter in England. He very kindly volunteered to lend us £2,000 and it didn't take us long to agree, aborting our plans to remain in England so we could head for a warmer clime. Duncan was organising this year's boys' trip, with Cuba as the destination. Stuart and I researched the surrounding countries and settled on Honduras as our own destination. We knew we'd have to work while we were away – the plane tickets would eat up over half of our newfound budget – but were sure we'd find a job at one of the many dive centres on Roatán Island.

Our home for the next three months would be in the town of West End on Roatán Island. The island is known as one of the best diving islands in the Caribbean, located near the Mesoamerican Barrier Reef, the second largest reef in the world after Australia's Great Barrier Reef. It took only a matter of days and a few heavy prayer sessions before we found ourselves renting a two-bedroom house, which stood ten feet off the ground and was rented to us by a local family. The timing was perfect: a Canadian couple had left the house a few days earlier and we knew that the universe was answering our prayers. We jumped happily at the opportunity, aware that it was an extremely rare find.

We soon settled into a routine, including collecting water in large containers from the shower tap, storing this precious commodity for evening showers and for cooking; water supply was limited as it ran through our pipes only a couple of hours every day. We will never forget one experience there, where our landlords came to warn us that we had to move out for a short time, taking all unsealed food packages with us. As he led us to the back of his boundary, we saw the ground moving, slowing coming towards us. Ants in their billions. Our landlord informed us that this has happened before, and the ants would swarm the house and then leave in four to five hours. We watched in amazement as our home became enveloped by the moving black carpet. On the plus side, it left the house spotless from crumbs and other insects.

Stuart and I immediately visited the dive shops in the area; we had paid upfront for our accommodation so now had less than $20 left in our savings. We searched for any openings for dive masters and Stuart was lucky to land a position at a backpackers' outfit called Reef Gliders. He worked there two days a week, relieving the full-time instructors and dive masters on their days off, earning a small amount of cash for his work plus the odd beer as a tip from the divers.

We realised we were in the perfect location: our accommodation was tucked away in a secure compound at the end of the popular tourist location of West End, an area teeming with hotels, dive shops, restaurants and bars. On exiting our new home we could turn right and head into the coastal beach town, or turn left and walk onto the sands of West Bay, a beautiful, quiet region with two resorts, one at each end of the bay, the closest one having a dock in front to secure the resort's parasailing boat.

Our budget was tight and we'd buy our food as the locals did, existing on a very basic diet and stopping the pick-up truck that sold fresh fruit and vegetables from the local area. We also made a little extra cash when we rented out our spare room for a week, connecting with a lovely Israeli girl called Shani. Stuart helped Shani get back in the water, as she had lost all her confidence on a dive and needed to regain her nerve. We loved our simple way of life and were so pleased to be in this tropical paradise, knowing how lucky we were to have landed on our feet in this ideal location.

One evening, as we sat on the nearby dock, admiring the colours of nature as the sun began to set on the horizon, we met Jim. He was our closest neighbour, as well as being the owner of the resort on the beach behind the dock, and the proprietor of the gleaming white 32-foot parasailing boat that was tied to the wooden rails beside us. We immediately connected with his larger-than-life personality and were soon introduced to his team of workers: Ken, the boat's hired captain, and Hazel, the parasailing assistant. Never having experienced this activity before, I jumped at the offer to go parasailing with Stuart the following day. Within 24 hours we found ourselves floating in the sky above the resort, attached to one another in a sitting position, dragged along by 800 feet of line behind the speedboat. The views of the white beaches and turquoise waters below were spectacular, and I was captivated as we flew at eye level with the peaked, jungle-draped mountains.

I was asked to work for this parasailing outfit over the next few weeks, as Hazel was needed elsewhere within the resort. I became a proficient deckhand, learning the skills necessary to get people up into the air safely, as well as assisting their cautious return onto the boat. Having enjoyed time on boats for most of my life, I was comfortable with my role, but I yearned to get back under water and continued my search for other work.

It wasn't long before I found my dream job, working part-time at the Luna Beach Resort, a high-class facility that offered diving to its wealthy guests. The resort was only a few minutes' walk from our front door, a lovely trek across the sands of West Bay. I began my Caribbean diving adventures, exploring the various underwater walls, wrecks, caverns and swim-throughs in the clear waters, all the while encountering a plethora of marine organisms, and all with fantastic visibility. The dive sites were incredible and our customers always left with smiles on their faces, tipping us handsomely for our services. Stuart would always tease me about the amount of cash I brought home, a far cry from his beer tips.

We had been on the island for over six weeks when we were joined by Tony and Adel. Adel would be my roommate while the boys were on their boys' trip to Cuba, and it was only a few days before the boys had packed their bags, ready to meet up with Duncan and Tim and explore the communist island.

Adel and I enjoyed a wonderful, chilled-out time while the boys were away, complementing each other in our household duties and making the most of our time on the beach and in the water. We camped out on the dock or on blow-up beds in the waters, creating a 'Motion Conservation Society' with those individuals that joined our regime, enforcing rules to conserve energy by performing as little movement as possible. We added one more to our team – a fellow traveller, Mike – who enjoyed our company and our ideals and joined us most days for our dock time. Our tans were deepening and I was grateful for the dive work – my six-pack was starting to become evident thanks to lifting the heavy dive tanks and to the healthy diet that was being forced on my system. Adel and I enjoyed great nights out, dancing the night away with our newfound friends and rejoicing in our connection, a sisterhood that would last a lifetime.

The month was soon up and Stuart was back, recounting tales of his adventures with the boys, describing a society that was completely different from our own. Cuba was not what he had expected. He had travelled all over the world visiting democratic countries, and was very impressed with how this communist country functioned. There were no homeless people – all citizens were provided with homes and food. The only negative he had experienced was that no one had the choice to become an entrepreneur; they all, from doctors to street cleaners, received basically the same wage. Stuart had come across a few individuals who were trying to make a bit of extra money, but at huge risk to themselves, with jail as the consequence. Our men found a guy who would take them scuba diving, pocketing the funds himself instead of the money going back to the central government. When the day for their dive arrived, the tanks were placed in a secret compartment under the car seats and the jackets, regulators and other dive gear were hidden in the door panels. This proved a necessary precaution as they were stopped multiple times at the police checks en route. Luckily, the diving equipment was not discovered. Stuart loved the country, both the people and the scenery, and enjoyed the epic street parties, fiestas that were like nothing he'd ever experienced.

With only a few weeks left on Roatán Island, Stuart started to search for other job opportunities – his part-time dive position at Reef Gliders had been filled in his absence – and took on the task of cleaning the undersides of boats in return for cash. After removing all the barnacles from the bottom of Jim's parasailing boat, Stuart agreed to clean a sailboat for Greg, a fellow traveller who had been exploring the Caribbean waters on his own and who was now part of our dock entourage. In exchange for Stuart's services, Greg took Stuart, Adel

Early childhood memories

Exploring Thailand, Laos, Vietnam and Cambodia with Ali and Margot

Meeting Stu, on the *Mama Hans* boat trip

... our tailor in Vietnam

Stunning Angkor Wat ...

... and on a squat toilet

Me spinning fire

Stuart aged about eight   Stuart working as a shepherd in Scotland

 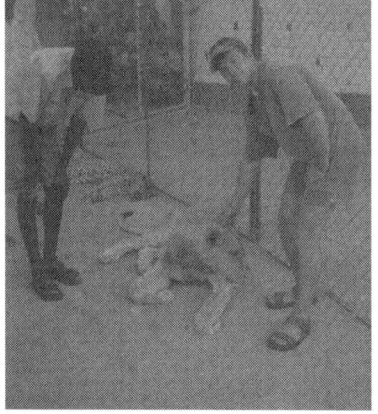

Tony, Duncan and Stu with cheetahs in Namibia ...
... and the lion starting to fixate on Stuart's shoe

Teaching children English in Thailand

Stuart just finishing a horse whisperer demonstration with a untrained horse

The Devon crew

The legendary Glastonbury

Me on my wedding day, flanked by my parents

Wedding posse enjoying Pasley

Me on Mount Cook, New Zealand

Victoria Falls

Storm approaching in Namibia

Heavenly Fiji

Some hair-raising experiences –
flash floods, and up close to a leopard

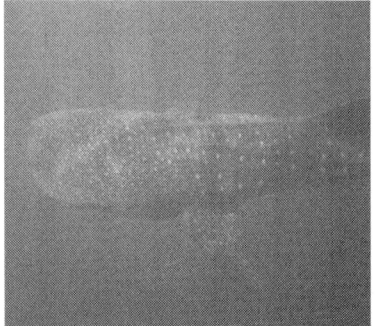

Close encounter with a whale shark

Bamboozi Beach, Mozambique

Close-up photos of a rhino with her calf, just before they charged

Mountain-boarding in Devon

Entering Batu Caves during Malaysian Hindu Festival

A tuk-tuk boat, Perhentian Island

A kadavi bearer, in a trance-like state and with sharpened hooks piercing the skin of his back

Barracuda and turtles in Borneo

Me working on the parasailing boat

Stuart and I – sunny days on Roatán Island

Me standing over Mayan Ball Court

My head in front of a Mayan Statue

My family

Stuart with Marie in Germany

Exploring Sri Lanka

Memories of Ethiopia, in the freezing heights of the mountains

Ethiopian tribeswomen, some with lip plates, and one with neck rings showing her rank in marriage

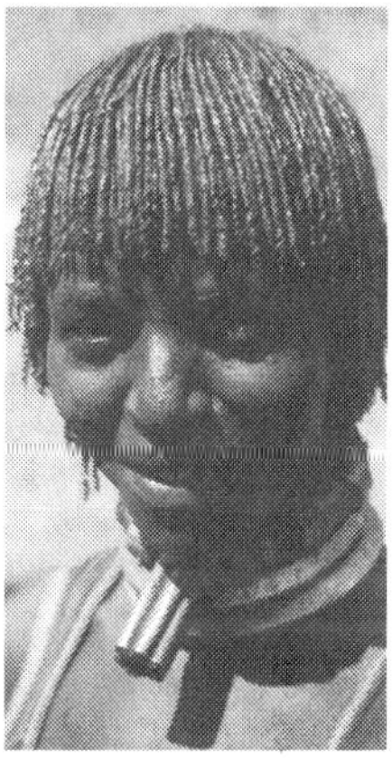

Kenya: a terrifying ride on a goat truck, and dancing with Masai warriors

Meeting a witch doctor and dancing with pygmies in Uganda

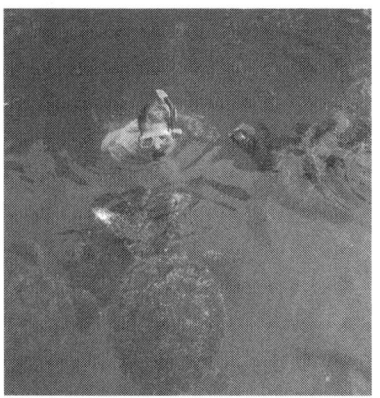 

Me swimming with turtles at Zanzibar Lagoon

A chilling monument to the slave trade, in Zanzibar, Tanzania

A giant silverback gorilla ... and a two-month-old colobus monkey

Stuart in Madagasgar

Family time in New Caledonia

My sisters and I celebrating Ali's wedding

Family time in Bali and Boracay

Memories of Panama, New York and beyond

I look forward to what our family will discover together on our future expeditions

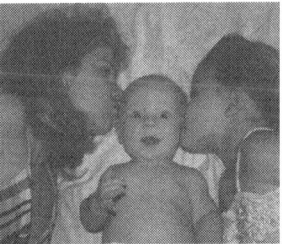

and me out on his boat, and we spent hours with the engines off, allowing the winds to fill the sails and propel us over the clear waters. We spent the afternoon drinking beer, chatting away as we gazed wistfully out over the Caribbean Sea, knowing that our time there was coming to an end.

We said farewell to Adel a few days later, then it wasn't long before we were also on the move. We were now headed to the Lake Yojoa district, bound for D&D Brewery, a guesthouse known for its beautiful surroundings and its amazing, hand-crafted beer. We stayed there for a week and were spoiled by its owner – Bob took us under his wing and showed us all the spectacular scenery that his region had to offer. From the lake and waterfalls to the caves and its geological gems, we enjoyed many days experiencing the beauty of Honduras and feeling the peace of nature.

We had one final stop to make before leaving the country: a visit to the archaeological site of Copán. A few thousand years ago, Copán had been a powerful Mayan city that had ruled over a vast kingdom. Now it was a ghost of its former self, barely hanging on to its ceremonial buildings and lavish works of art as the surrounding jungle attempted to break them away. We learned how, at its height, over a 400-year span, 16 kings had used their political and military power to rule, controlling Copán's people with their Mayan ways, building and rebuilding religious structures, until the city had fallen into ruin and become overrun by the surrounding vegetation. Centuries later the city was rediscovered and, as we stood now in this deserted historic site, we were blown away by what had been left behind, especially by the Mayan Ball Court and the Petroglyph Staircase. This stone staircase, constructed on the side of a 30-metre high pyramidal structure, and made of stone blocks displaying 2,200 petroglyphs, formed the single longest hieroglyphic text ever found in pre-Columbian America. Simply amazing! The Ball Court, a rectangular area flanked by two elongated pyramids, was where Mayan warriors played their sacred and fierce ball game, often to the death.

Seeing such amazing ancient architecture and hearing of the lifestyles of these people made me appreciate the past, but also made me thankful for the fact that I had been born in the 'modern world', where sacrifices to appease the gods were not commonplace and our lives were not ruled by the fancies of one individual. But then again, some of the most modern countries have crazy dictators or religiously fanatical leaders, so have we really changed that much? Hmmm, food for thought.

Chapter 12
PIG and a Holy Pilgrimage

We were moving house. We had returned from our Central American adventures and now moved our belongings into a mobile home, a type of housing I had never dreamed I would live in, but one that ticked all the boxes for us for now. Our new home was positioned on the farm belonging to the father of Stuart's boss, the location that housed all the livestock and machinery for the Sheep Show.

My recruitment agency had found a long-term placement for me while I was away. I was soon back at work, this time at a school that was different from my past experiences – it was on a council estate and brought in a different type of student. The children had attitudes that were new to me, answering my questions about their life ambitions with responses like, 'Going on the dole'. It took me some time to figure out that this meant they intended to exist on unemployment benefits, a situation I had always assumed was only for when someone needed assistance between jobs, never thinking that people would be able to take these hand-outs indefinitely. I was also shocked by the lack of parental support – I was often verbally abused, for example, when I phoned a student's home to enquire about homework not being completed, and I heard many similar stories from my fellow teachers. I'd watch as other supply teachers were bullied and harassed – the children didn't take well to new faces at their school – and heard more than one of those teachers saying that they would refuse to return to the school in the future. I was lucky: with my foreign accent and alternative lifestyle, the students responded well to me and would force one another to behave in order to hear stories of my global adventures.

Stuart popped in and out of my life, driving the artic show truck across the UK to perform the Sheep Show at various fetes and country fairs. He'd return for just a day or two, before packing his belongings and setting off again, sometimes having to stay away for as long as three weeks as he went from show to show in the peak of the season.

When school was let out for summer vacation, I returned for my annual visit to Canada. I wanted to be there for the first weekend of August, a weekend reserved for PIG, the Pasley Island Games. Just about all the inhabitants would meet in the morning in the centre of the island for a variety of events, such as track events, three-legged races, water-balloon tosses and tug-of- wars, pitching North Bay members against South Bay members, with the fight for the mighty trophy in the back of every competitor's mind, children and adults alike. These morning events were then always brought to a close with a candy-stuffed piñata, with children flinging themselves on to the ground, trying to claim as many of the falling sweets as possible. In the evening we'd all gather together in either North or South Bay; the location to host the dinner and dance alternated each year, with the Bay's members pulling together to create a fantastic evening. We'd then party until the early hours of the morning, enjoying the company of families who had been on this island for generations, dancing with both young and old and loving the closeness of our community. On Sunday islanders came together for swimming competitions and raft races for the kids, as well as a team triathlon and a long-distance swim for the older generation. All in all a fun-packed weekend not to be missed.

When I returned from my Canadian holiday, I had an amazing surprise waiting for me: Stuart had bought me a car! It felt great to have my own set of wheels – I loved my little Vauxhall Corsa and the freedom of not having to share a car every time I needed to get somewhere.

With a month to go before the end of this stint in the UK, we started to make plans for the six months of travel ahead, knowing that we would also need to put in some family time. We were thrilled when we had bought our round-the-world tickets, relieved that we would be escaping the UK winter. At the end of the work season we flew to Germany to visit Stuart's daughter, after which we drove to Devon, where we reconnected with our great mates Marci and Blue, Adel and Tony, and our long-time work mates Ian and Phoebe.

After a week with them it was time for our six-month holiday, and we boarded our flight to cross the Atlantic, bound for Vancouver. We spent eight weeks there, including the Christmas period, and moved from one family to another, ensuring we had quality time with all our close relatives and friends. We were able to have fun on Whistler Mountain, snowboarding down the slopes with Amber and Ali, then returning to Amber's chalet for evenings of debauchery. I was also able to get away with Sarah and Weeze; after organising a girls' weekend down in Seattle, we had a fabulous time shopping, eating and enjoying each other's company. We attended numerous pre-Christmas parties and enjoyed Christmas Day with the family, my first in their new home on Bowen. We relished the roaring fire and the sound of carols, and watched from the windows as snow fell on the dark-green forest.

Although there were so many enjoyable aspects to our stay, we realised that this was not the best time of year to spend in Canada. The rainy month of November, followed by the cold, wet and short days of December, resulted in many housebound days, which drove my husband insane. Stuart got headaches from staying indoors for too long, and we'd have to go for walks in the torrential rains just to get some fresh air. Most people worked Monday to Friday, and I realised that summer was a much better time to visit my friends and family in Canada.

It felt a welcome release when we flew across the Pacific at the beginning of January to join our New Zealand family for their summer holidays. We accompanied various family members on different camping adventures, going on mountainside hikes and spending days kayaking, fishing and swimming in the beautiful rivers and lakes in the region. Then we all descended on Wanaka, a gorgeous town situated at the foot of a lake and surrounded by the peaks of the Southern Alps. Louise was completing her first triathlon there and we all cheered her on, holding banners in the air and screaming at the top of our lungs as she passed by.

My parents had joined us in order to explore the South Island and in the weeks that followed I became their guide, driving them from the southerly Milford Sound fjord to the northerly tip of Golden Bay. We stayed in wonderful B&Bs as we explored the perimeter of the island, stopping to view all the natural wonders along the way. It was at this time that I finally introduced my parents to my adopted New

Zealand parents, Helen and Clarry, who welcomed us lovingly into their seaside home.

Around this time Stuart and I bought our second house, aware of the growth of the city of Invercargill. It took us less than a week to find and purchase a new property there, financed by the wonderful people at the bank, who were happy to lend us more money as we were paying the first house off in such large instalments.

Our time in Stuart's homeland flew by and it was soon time to board our flight, with Indonesia as our first destination. I had been to 'Indo' before but never with Stuart, and I wanted him to experience the laid-back atmosphere of the Gili Islands, situated between the main islands of Bali and Lombok. It wasn't long before we found suitable accommodation and exchanged our travel clothes for our swimsuits, delighted to feel the powdery white sand between our toes as we explored the beaches, before jumping into the turquoise-tinted, bath-warm waters. The freedom was exhilarating and we felt blessed to be together in such a gorgeous setting. We had signed up on a ten-dive package that gave us the use of a glitzy resort's facilities, our main focus being on its luxurious pool and cushioned deck loungers.

The island prohibited motorised traffic, so we made our way around on foot, discovering private beaches and setting up camp each day. We positioned our hammocks amongst the trees and bushes that hugged the shores, enjoying the best views from these reclined positions. On other days we'd go out on dives, exploring the deepwater coral reefs, swimming beside sharks, rays and other marine life, and we felt completely at ease in the depths as we toured the underwater sites. In the evenings we'd settle ourselves at one of the many seaside restaurants, reclining on the large cushions that encircled the tables, befriending fellow backpackers and enjoying the tales that flowed.

When our time was up we felt fully relaxed and ready to move on to our journey's end, a month in Sri Lanka. We had chosen this destination on the advice of Gill, who was our landlord in the UK and Stuart's boss's mother. She had been born in Sri Lanka and spent many years in the country before her family moved to England, and her tales of all the gorgeous landscapes and the myriad captivating cultures had enticed us to include Sri Lanka in our itinerary. We had even booked a one-week tour with Lal, a local friend of hers.

This would be the first time in all our travels where, on exiting the baggage-reclaim area of the airport, we looked for our names on one of the placards held up by the people meeting new arrivals. We zeroed in on our tour guide, Lal, who directed us to the lovely, air-conditioned van he had waiting for us. Lal told us all about this amazing country; about its rich history, which spanned over 3,000 years; and its diversity when it came to religions, ethnicities and languages. I would learn that, because of its geographical location, at the southern tip of India, combined with its naturally deep harbours, this country had been strategically important from the time of the ancient Silk Road through to World War II. Sri Lanka's past, the main theme of which was its rich history in the Buddhist faith, was brought to life as we were driven across the diverse landscape.

We left the capital, Colombo, and drove inland. We passed hillsides enveloped by tea plantations, watching as women worked the fields, carrying baskets strapped to their backs or on top of their heads, and waving as we passed. The first stop on our tour was the sacred Temple of the Tooth in the historic city of Kandy, one of Buddhism's most sacred relics, and one that draws followers of the Buddhist faith from all over the world. The royal complex is situated around Kandy's lake, and it was within this breathtaking setting that I would learn of Sri Lanka's rich Buddhist heritage and the fact that the first-known Buddhist writings had been composed on this island.

After Kandy we drove north to the cave temples of Dambulla, the island's most popular historic site and the centre of pilgrimage over the past 22 centuries, for Buddhists and Hindus alike. The cave monastery is crammed with Buddhist statues, including a 15-metre long, reclining Buddha. The walls and ceiling, decorated with vividly coloured frescoes, together form the largest antique painted surface in the world. I was blown away by the exquisite 2,000-year-old murals depicting the life and times of the Lord Buddha, the detail of the murals making me appreciate the exquisite craftsmanship of his worshippers. The setting drew me in, forcing me to analyse my own beliefs and those that had been there for centuries, and as I walked around the golden statues and passed the incredible frescoes, I tried to absorb all the positive aspects of the Buddhist faith, which Stuart was already a big fan of.

Within a few hours we were en route to a nearby rock citadel, a dramatic tourist attraction that furnishes the remains of a fifth-century palace, perched on the summit of the vertiginous Lion Rock. Known as Sigiriya, this citadel represents an astonishing feat of engineering and construction: the royal palace is set on top of a massive rock with a flattened summit and rises 200 metres above the forested plain. The site was incredible and we couldn't begin to guess how they had been able to piece it together, shaking our heads in awe as we left the area.

After a day of touring, Lal brought us to a guesthouse, where we would be spoiled by the culinary talents of our host, being served a multitude of gastronomic delights. The cuisine had some similarities with that of the country's closest neighbour, India, due to its close proximity, and had been influenced by other foreign traders, who since ancient times had brought their native fares to Sri Lanka. The resulting dishes were exquisite, becoming some of my favourite food in the world, and, from breakfast through to dinner, I always looked forward to our meal times.

We continued our tour along the southern edge of the hill country and stopped at one of the most striking natural landmarks, the soaring summit of Adam's Peak. As one of the most celebrated places of pilgrimage, the mountain had accumulated a mass of legends centred around the curious depression at its summit, the 'Sacred Footprint'. The original Buddhist story claims that this is the footprint of Buddha himself. Muslims, meanwhile, claim it to be the footprint of Adam, who is said first to have set foot on earth after being cast out of heaven, and who stood on the mountain's summit on one leg in penitence until his sins were forgiven. And finally, according to Hindu tradition, the footprint was created by their own god, Shiva.

Despite all these rival claims, Adam's Peak remains an essentially Buddhist place of worship, an object of pilgrimage for over a thousand years, and Lal now informed us that it was our turn to complete the sacred climb. I was full of cold and wasn't overjoyed by the prospect of the arduous ascent, especially after hearing that it was customary to start the journey in the middle of the night. But, after some deliberation, I agreed to go on my very first pilgrimage.

I was cold and tired as we set off at 2 am from our guesthouse, but I soon warmed up as we made headway down the track. Being here during the main pilgrimage season meant that we would pass all sorts of groups, from old grandmothers to parents carrying their infants, all making their way along the sacred track. This enabled me to focus on the profound meaning of this journey rather than on my dreadful cold. After trekking 7 kilometres and climbing 5,400 steps, we reached the summit in time for dawn, witnessing the extraordinary, cloud-free views and glimpsing the peak's enigmatic shadow. As we sat huddled close together, individuals from all around the world, we could feel the peace radiating from this stunning landscape and I felt in awe of our earth and humbled by the experience. The fluttering of the colourful peace flags could be heard whipping in the wind, and soon, as our bodies cooled down after the challenging climb, we were forced to focus on the chilly temperatures of the altitude. It was time to return to our hotel.

During the final days of our tour we drove south and visited an elephant sanctuary, as well as embarking on a safari in Yala National Park, home to one of the world's densest populations of leopards. We were thrilled when we came upon one of the beautiful cats hidden among the bush. It sat so still, silent and perfectly camouflaged within the shadows of the branches, and we turned our engine off so that we could admire its grace. After several minutes, the leopard sprinted away and we continued our tour. We spied many other forms of wildlife, including the Sri Lankan elephant, water buffalo and hundreds of bird species, and when the day was over we left the park with beaming smiles on our faces. Sri Lanka is among the top five biodiversity hotspots in the world, and after spending hours in this park, we could understand why. This was the perfect ending to a great tour and we were very thankful to Lal for being our wonderful tour guide and host.

Since we still had a few weeks to spare, we asked to be dropped off at one of the southerly beaches, to allow us to chill out in Mirissa and Hikadua. These are quiet stretches of coastline, which had been scarred by the Asian tsunami – large sections of beachfront had been swept away by the receding waters. We dived for $12 each, our cheapest dives to date, but were not overly impressed by the dive sites – the reefs were stripped bare and lacked marine life. We swam and walked, enjoying the last days of our holiday, and always looking forward to meal times.

Unfortunately, during this time we kept hearing reports of deaths due to the fighting that was taking place in the north of the country. Sri Lanka was still involved in Asia's longest modern civil war, a clash that arose due to ethnic tensions between the Buddhist Sinhalese majority and the mainly Hindu Tamil minority. The locals were not shocked by the news reports; the fight had stretched out over the past two decades, killing up to 80,000 and forcing hundreds of thousands to be uprooted, as well as creating thousands of child soldiers and resulting in the laying of at least one million mines. No wonder these acts were said to have scarred the nation. Our concern grew as we heard that the Tamil Tigers had taken to the skies and had performed their first bombing raid near the international airport; we could feel the tension in the air as we entered the capital ready for our departure.

As we flew away from this beautiful country, known as the 'Pearl of the Indian Ocean', we marvelled at its rich history and diversity of religions, and were saddened that modern differences of ethnicities could cause such hardships and devastation for so many. The Buddhist philosophy of leading a moral life, being mindful and aware of your own thoughts and actions and developing wisdom and understanding, didn't seem to come into play when it came to this terrible civil conflict. I found myself taking a hard look at whether any religion in the world stood above the rest, in terms of bringing peace and solidarity to the human race.

Chapter 13
Running for Our Lives

My husband was being held captive in Scotland. It was August 2007 and I heard the details of Stuart's confinement when I phoned him from Canada. Men wearing white biohazard suits and masks had descended on Stuart's show truck in the middle of the night, immediately quarantining him and his show sheep, and then moving him to a restricted area surrounded by a six-foot perimeter fence, preventing him from moving on to his next show.

This impoundment did at least have one positive outcome: Stuart was now becoming famous! He had been interviewed by a variety of newspapers; he'd done radio interviews for stations around the world, including his homeland of New Zealand; and articles headlining his story had been broadcast on the BBC and ITV, leading UK television channels.

A foot-and-mouth outbreak had struck the UK and, due to its potentially massive economic impact, the government was doing everything it could to contain it. The disease was caused by a highly infectious virus that affected cloven-hoofed farm animals, and movement of all sheep, cattle and pigs had been put on standstill. I had been in England in 2001, when the previous outbreak had occurred, and could remember the burning pyres of dead carcasses dotted around the Devon landscape, filling our nostrils with their disgusting fumes. At that time the disease had resulted in the slaughtering of over seven million animals, causing devastation for many farms and rural businesses, and it was clear the government wanted at all costs to avoid a repetition of that situation. So my husband was impounded in Scotland, and could be stuck there for several weeks.

After Stuart and the animals were finally released from their impoundment, it was obvious that the Sheep Show business was going to be severely restricted for the remainder of the season, due to the constraints to livestock movement. Wanting to help to keep the business alive, Stuart suggested incorporating a new show, one that he had already presented for years and which did not involve hoofed animals. Hence, the Dog and Duck Show was brought to life. This was a side venture, a business that Stuart could call his own, one that was close to Stuart's heart and encompassed his passion for canines.

After I returned from Canada, it wasn't long before we were sitting with our heads together, looking at the globe and making our decisions on where to go for our next six-month holiday. Africa was drawing us back and we became excited as we created our itinerary: Ethiopia, Kenya, Uganda, Tanzania and Madagascar.

We couldn't book our plane tickets until we heard from Tony, this year's boys' trip destination co-ordinator. When we received his phone call, our immediate response to his chosen country was, 'Where in the world is Djibouti?' We knew that Tony had probably settled on the location by planting his finger on the spinning globe, so we decided to investigate this unheard-of place before buying our tickets. Stuart and I learned that Djibouti was one of the tiniest, youngest and least-known nations in Africa, perched on the Horn of Africa and sharing borders with Eritrea, Ethiopia and Somalia.

Although there were articles about the islands, beaches and mountainous regions of the country, it was also one of the most expensive places in the world to visit, with a typical day in the capital costing over US$225. This couldn't be the right setting for the three amigos, and it wasn't long before Tony came back with option 2: Eritrea.

Eritrea was a different kettle of fish. Our research on this new destination showed that it had a very violent history. It was currently involved in deathly border disputes with its sworn enemy and neighbour, Ethiopia, and its tourism revenues made up less than one per cent of the country's GDP – a number not likely to grow, as the country was hampered by drought, political instability and war. Less than a decade earlier, Eritrean–Ethiopian border clashes had developed into a full-scale war, in which 70,000 people were killed. And these clashes continued to the present, with border towns being claimed by both sides. The UN had tried to assist, implementing ceasefire and peace agreements in 2000. But these were now being disregarded, and the local government was ordering UN mission members to depart the country.

Eritrea wasn't able to provide enough food for its people – two-thirds of its population were receiving food aid. And there seemed to be no end in sight; economic progress was hampered by the proportion of Eritreans who were in the army rather than the workforce. All in all, not a great place to visit, and we phoned Tony again with the news.

Third time lucky: Tony settled now on northern Ethiopia, informing us that it was now the starting point of his own itinerary; he and Adel were going to visit Ethiopia, Kenya, Uganda and Tanzania on their four-month holiday together. It took Stuart and me a few days to get comfortable with the idea, knowing that we'd all be travelling together throughout these four African countries, and that the days of travel on the African soils would no doubt be challenging. It was a big step for two couples to be together 24/7 for a number of months, and we hoped that it wouldn't fracture our friendship.

But at least we now had a plan. The three boys flew to Ethiopia a month ahead of us, while we three girls flew to the Canary Islands for a two-week girls' trip. Adel and I stayed in one room, and Wendy (Duncan's 'better half') and her new baby girl, Miki, stayed in the room next door. We hired a car and drove around the tourist roads of Tenerife, returning to our resort to swim in the pool and work on our tans. We had a lovely holiday, full of girl-power talks, great food and chill-out time, and returned to England refreshed and ready for our next big adventure. Ethiopia here we come!

23 November 2007: Today is the day. Five years married and I couldn't be happier. Stu and I are sitting in Addis Ababa, the capital of Ethiopia, enjoying a bottle of Jacobs Creek Reserve Shiraz, celebrating our five years of marriage. Five wonderful years of marriage.

With my dad having voiced doubts on our union, giving us a five-year time limit, we loved the fact that we had proved him wrong and that we were stronger than ever. We looked back at our time together and felt proud at what we had accomplished – we had great jobs awaiting us in England, two properties under our belt, and were still taking six months off each year to travel the world. It was exciting to be back in each other's arms, and we promised to continue to love, cherish and support one another, forever and always.

We remained in Addis Ababa for a few days, making plans in terms of what we wanted to see and where we wanted to go, while adapting to the heat and getting used to the fact that, with our white skin, we stood out like sore thumbs wherever we went. Just before Duncan left, we all went out for a great dinner where we shared buckets of beer, laughing our heads off as the men described the highlights of their boys' adventures in the north of the country. They had been forced to hire a 'guard' to travel with them as they hiked the northerly national park, due to the area being designated a war zone, with the fighting with Eritrea still a threat. They were in search of the Ethiopian wolf, the only wolf species to be found in Africa, and known to be the most threatened canid in the world. But they had to laugh when they met their chaperone, a 65-year-old hill man armed with an ancient, single-shot musket, and who didn't speak a word of English. The boys joked that, if they ever did get into trouble, throwing rocks over the musket would be more effective than trying to shoot from it.

Then it was our turn to leave the capital, headed for our first stop, the walled city of Harar in Eastern Ethiopia.

Yesterday we took an 11-hour bus journey from the capital, Addis Ababa, to Harar. When Stu and Tony bought the tickets, they were told that the bus left at 5 am, so we all got up at 4 am and were at the bus station by 4.45 am. Then we waited and waited and waited ... standing outside in the cold, waiting for bus #2197, while other buses poured out exhaust fumes in our direction as they came and went. Then around 6.45 we were told that our bus had broken down and wouldn't be coming, and we were to get on a full bus that had already been boarded by stampeding passengers 20 minutes earlier. Oh no! We girls were instructed not to wait in line but to push ourselves onto the bus, while the boys handled the bags. So Adel and I boarded, only to find the bus completely full. Jam-packed. Luckily, one of the workers, who wore a distinctive green suit, directed us to the back row and got an old man with his suitcase to move out ... as Westerners we have more rights than the elderly. Not good, but we just didn't feel comfortable refusing the seats. So we sat. It felt like the whole morning passed before the bus finally started moving.

Once we were out of the city we passed through flat lands, watching camels, oxen and goats being led by small boys, and making a game out of counting the number of car wrecks on the side of the road. At one point we saw 20–30 vultures pulling an animal apart, their winged movements and loud squawking attracting more of their kind. Later we witnessed an injured camel, which had obviously caused a car accident, sitting forlornly at the edge of the pavement. And there were so many Ethiopians, in all states: from impoverished, apparently homeless people, to others beautifully attired in fine suits.

We stopped for five minutes, grabbed a couple of samosas, then drove on, this time through the mountain regions. Mountain after mountain, we crossed their flanks, scaling their heights then slowly braking our way down their slopes, only to repeat the process again and again. Luckily, we had a 20-minute lunch break where we were able to go to the toilet, but the rule of the day was ... DO NOT DRINK.

After some confusion as to where we needed to get off the bus, we drove into Harar as the sun set and the huge moon looked on. We were warned to watch our stuff and then started walking in the direction of Tana Hotel, which we had learned from Lonely Planet had hot showers *and cost only $5 per day. After being followed for five minutes by four guys, each saying he wanted to be our guide, we caught a* tuk-tuk *to the hotel, and thank God we did – it was at least 2 km out of town, all uphill! When we arrived the music was blaring, the restaurant was heaving and a football match was on. We went to the reception and asked for two rooms, only to be told the hotel was full ('Ah!'). But we were finally led to two rooms, one upstairs and the other downstairs. Tony and Adel went downstairs, Stu and I went up, only to be informed that the room downstairs had a squat toilet and no hot water. Well, we had a hot water tank, but it took some time to warm up. Stu tried to be a plumber and trick the system to heat more quickly, and in the process electrocuted himself. JESUS – that could have been really bad, with water all over the floor.*

So, with no hot water (yet), it was time to try and feed our hungry tummies. After struggling to find a table in the packed restaurant, we at last found one and sat down to a meal of meat, bread and spaghetti. And so here we are, sitting at a table in the middle of Harar, standing out like sore thumbs as everyone else is as black as black can be. While looking at our neighbouring tables and their food, Adel stands up and goes to talk to a group behind us, asking what they are eating. Meat and bread – the speciality. And they offer us all a taste. Adel (a long-time vegetarian) and I decline, but Tony goes in for a bite and loves it. So we sit down again ... and again another neighbouring table grabs our attention and offers us food. How kind. We thankfully decline, but think: if we were back in our own countries, and a group of foreigners came and asked us what we were eating, would we ever offer food from our plates?

Being here makes you think.

When you hear of all the refugees from Eritrea, abandoned in refugee camps with hundreds of thousands of others, stuck in the middle of nowhere, not allowed to work, not allowed to make money; their survival dependent on the tiny purses of the agencies in charge of the camps, and their families back home charged US$5,000 because one of their family members has fled military conscription and escaped to another country.

And when you hear of stories of people from Somalia, Sudan and Eritrea, all seeking a better life away from their war-torn countries, coming to Ethiopia to find a semblance of life, only to find their hands tied when they can't find a livelihood, can't make a wage, in a country that has two major catastrophes a year: the winter floods, which make roads impassable and steal the nutrients from the earth as they overflow the landscape, and the summer droughts, where rain doesn't fall for months, bakes the earth and turns it to dust ... and they have no reserves. That's one of the problems: no infrastructure. No storage tanks for water. No sewage system. Frequent blackouts due to power failures. No food. No money.

These are just some of the types of problems faced by so many of the Ethiopian population, and it seemed clear that the people sharing the restaurant with us this evening led very basic lives. And yet these kind citizens were asking US if we wanted some of their food. We felt truly humbled.

This was a life lesson that stood out for me. These individuals forced me to reassess my values, briefly touching my life to steer me in a better direction, and I have since that night endeavoured to be more hospitable to anyone I meet.

We had come to Harar with a mission in mind. After a good night's sleep, we packed our belongings and moved to a hotel within 100 metres of the gates of the walled town and within walking distance of the famed hyenas. These wild animals had a special connection with some of the local families, and we were aware of the rich history between these dramatically different species of mammals.

We had learned that Ethiopia had been in a very dark place in the early twentieth century: it was in the middle of a war with Italy, as well as being hit by plague. The people of Harar were dying left, right and centre from plague and famine, and wild packs of spotted hyenas (the largest of their kind, with some of the strongest jaws of the entire animal kingdom) had learned to scavenge and feed off the dead human bodies. This went on for many years. The problem for the hyenas started when the plague had subsided and there were no more bodies to scavenge: their food source had dissipated. But these animals had become so comfortable in the town that they started to realise that there were other options, and they began to terrorise the young and the elderly. As people became scared to leave their houses after dark due to the prowling animals, two different families on either side of the town came up with a plan to help. The families would take wheelbarrows to all the different butchers, collecting all the bones that they could find. They then took the bones to the outside wall and dumped them there for the hyenas to feast on. After some time, certain members of those families would sit away from the bones, watching the hyenas come and go, unaware of the connection that they were creating between themselves and the wild animals. Later, those people would sit closer and closer to the bones, as the hyenas were becoming more and more comfortable with them. The humans then started to throw pieces of meat to the hyenas, which progressed to feeding them by hand, until eventually they could feed them from their mouths. This was a true acceptance from a wild species. Similar remarkable stories have happened only a handful of times in human history, where wild animals have accepted humans as members of their pack. The hyena story still continues today, as it was passed on from generation to generation, and we were here to see it.

So we moved hotels, dropped off our gear, and began our stroll through the old city. We were immediately surrounded and followed by a number of children who said that they could be our guides, as well as one of them saying that he was the son of the hyena man, so could get us a good deal. We thanked them but said we'd like just to wander the streets; they said 'no problem' but continued to follow us for the duration of the walk.

That evening, after being continually pestered by a guy at our hotel who wanted to be our guide and also take us to the hyenas, we walked out on our own, in the direction of the hyena feeding. Along the way, an Ethiopian guy helped us with directions and, just as the sun was setting, we arrived at a clearing where we saw three men on the rocks overlooking the distant landscape, calling out to the hyenas to come for dinner. Within five minutes we could see their shapes start to materialise through the brush – they were coming!!! Luckily there was a French couple in a hired jeep there as well; as the dark settled, they turned on their lights and we were able to see the spectacle clearly.

The main Ethiopian, the 'top dog', sat down with a large basket and proceeded to take out strips of meat, which he placed at the ends of twigs and offered to the animals. There were six hyenas and we could see that they were really comfortable with the man who was feeding them. He sat cross-legged on a mat and the hyenas came up, at first tentatively, and then with more confidence, and took the meat offered from the stick. After several minutes the man welcomed us to come forward, one at a time, and feed the hyenas ourselves! Stu, Tony, Adel and I took it in turns to go forward and, with cameras flashing, fed the animals. Unfortunately, a truck went by before I fed them, and the resulting dust in the air ruined all the pictures of me with the hyenas. So later that night we decided we'd repeat the experience the next day. We came away from this evening's experience buzzing, still in shock from how close we'd come to the hyenas. UNBELIEVABLE!

The next day we wandered through the old city again and found a barber for Stu. While I waited, I met a 33-year-old Ethiopian man, Abdi Hassen, a fellow biology teacher. We had a great conversation about Ethiopia, about what it meant to be a Muslim in this country. He told me how he wanted to meet a white girl to marry as they were 'much more open to life and sexual intercourse', and about how, even with his monthly wage of Br 1800 (very high, compared with the average daily wage of Br 10 (= \$1US) per day), he would never be able to travel like us since his wage only just covered his living costs. We talked about poverty and how the government spent money on weapons and war rather than looking after its people. We even talked about climate change and global warming. It was a great discussion with a local man, and we exchanged handshakes and smiles as we parted.

That evening, we all went to the other hyena man – there were two places to see them – and came across an old guy sitting on a piece of cardboard. It started more slowly this time as we were just outside the wall of the old city and on a road with a lamppost not too far away. As the man called and called, we could hear the hyenas 'laughing' in the distance. Eventually they came closer, but just as they approached, an oncoming vehicle raced down the track, throwing up dust and causing the hesitant animals to shy back into the woods.

After more time, a lot of hollering, and plenty of bones and food thrown out on to the roads, the animals appeared. It was time to move in and take some pictures. As I sat with the old man, a 'rogue' hyena came in and started fighting with another hyena right beside me. The dust flew as their angry yelping tore through the air. I was a little tentative feeding the animals by hand after witnessing such a ferocious fight, and didn't feed them with a stick in my mouth as the others had. But what an experience. Amazing!

The next day was our last in this city, and we enjoyed ourselves as we walked along the narrow dirt roads, buying wool blankets for our next adventure and eating samosas at the main boulevard café. After a 4 am wake-up, we walked to the bus station, bought our return tickets to the capital and waited for our bus. This time we didn't have to fight for our seats, but it would be a very long journey as we endured eight 'custom stops', where all passengers had to show their ID (a lengthy process), as well as three stops when the bus broke down. What had been a ten-hour trip from Addis Ababa to Harar now became a 15-hour return journey. A day where we couldn't drink, and where we seemed to stop every hour for some reason or another. A very long day!

I'm writing this at 4,000 metres. It's harder to breathe up here and feels like everything I do requires exertion. Wow, so much stuff has transpired since our last adventure. We are now on Day 4 of our Bale

National Park experience. We are a group of six, who started in Addis Ababa with the idea of going to Bale Park for six days. We shopped, we organised, we took a bus that left at 6 am to Dinsho (160 km) and travelled over unpaved, potholed terrain for 152 km at 20 km/h, arriving at our destination at 4 pm. We decided against staying in the brothel-type accommodation available in the village, and hired some guys to help us with our packs. Acting like Sherpas, they led us to the headquarters of the park, and we ended up at the most amazing campsite. The couple we added to our group are Lorena (Italian) and Dez (Irish).

Today is Friday 7 December 2007. We are at the final campsite and just packing down, ready for a hot shower and clean clothes. It has been an incredible journey. We're ready to move on, but look back at this experience with a sense of accomplishment. On the first day of our trek, we left our campsite at the headquarters (which was amazing for animals ... we saw loads of kudus, dik-diks, bushbucks and jackals) and walked 14 km to our first campsite. Along the way we passed small communities, each consisting of three to five wooden houses. Often the kids would run out screaming 'farangi' – their word for 'foreigner'. It was a great walk, quite fast, but we all managed it, and at the end we spotted three Ethiopian wolves!!! This was really cool.

The campsite was close to the wolves' den, and there was a male and a female that were trying to break away from the main pack. They hung around the hills beside our campsite. The BBC were there and had access to the only firewood and building, so we all went to bed early and FROZE in our tents! Stu got up early and joined one of the researchers as he left for the Ethiopian wolves' den. As the sun's rays touched the frozen ground, he saw a family of wolves, adults and young, stretching as they came out to meet the new day. On his solo walk back, he came across three other wolves and got some amazing photos, describing how he had read the terrain and positioned himself in front of them, within a few metres of the track. After Stu had left that morning I stayed awake and watched as two local wolves crossed the valley towards me and walked right on by, about 30 feet away! Incredible! There was ice on the inside of the tent and on my sleeping bag and hair, and it was pretty uncomfortable ... such are the joys of camping.

Day 2: We hiked for 17 km and saw more wolves and klipspringers (antelopes). It was a beautiful walk with spectacular views: valleys, mountains, rock formations. Spectacular! The second campsite was in a valley, with a meandering stream to one side, and a hill with large boulders behind us. We all picked a rock to set our tents up behind. And tonight we had a roaring fire!

Day 3: A walk of 20 km, up, up, up to 4,100 m, where we hired horses for a few hours and admired the beauty that surrounded us. We ended up at a campsite on the side of a plateau, close to a small village with four houses. Even with a campfire we were freezing. The zip on Dez and Lorena's tent was broken, so the wind just blew in and froze them. Stu and I shared body heat but still had an uncomfortable sleep. We woke up to frost and ice all around us and in our tents, but the scenery was so incredible, with massive oblong boulders as a backdrop and an incredible plateau in front of us – landscape that I had never seen before. It felt like we were on another planet. The clouds were flying past us, as we stood above them, as the plateau was over 4000m in altitude (12,000 feet). There was one local family that resided in this crazy landscape, who came out with milk and eggs for sale, so we indulged and had a lovely breakfast.

Day 4: Today was supposed to be a flat, three-hour walk, but turned out to be a steady incline up various hills, for five hours! But we couldn't complain – the campsite was situated on the side of a hill, with a beautiful view of the lake, and with local wolves as our neighbours. This day's walk was 17 km.

Day 5: We woke up refreshed after a warm night's sleep (having pitched our tent on cow manure), and packed our bags so our porters could take them to the final campsite. We stayed behind with the kettle, fire, shampoo and conditioner, and all washed our hair for the first time in five days! What a relief! When we were all clean (except for our clothes, which are vile), we walked the final five km to our final campsite. We made it!

Overall it was a breathtakingly beautiful trek. We'll all look back on it with smiles on our faces.

Whenever I think of our Bale Park Adventure, I'll remember:

1) The dust and dirt that we accumulated, day after day

2) The freezing nights, with the cold seeping up from the ground, having to huddle together with Stu, and waking up with aching hips and sore lower back. And the freezing evenings, where I tried to stay warm by wearing every article of clothing in my possession. Definitely not for the fashion-conscious!

3) Always having to watch my feet while I walked, because of the thousands of holes made by the mole rats and other rodents

4) The unbelievable scenery

5) The endangered Ethiopian Wolves – the rarest of all canines

6) Being a super-hero part of 'Team International' and trekking for hours every day

On to the next adventure …

It was during these five days of trekking that I found a new love, for it was the first time in my life that I would drink coffee. I was shocked when we walked into a small mud hut to find an Italian coffee machine and, because of the cold due to the high elevation, I accepted the macchiato that was offered, adding four scoops of sugar to mask the taste. I fell in love with this hot liquid – it gave me a rush of energy (no doubt due mainly to the amount of sugar I'd added) and warmed my chilled body. The Italians had invaded Ethiopia in the past and then been sent packing, and I was grateful that they had left some things behind, the best one being their love of making great coffee.

We had accomplished our quest to find the Ethiopian wolf, listed as the most threatened canid in the world, with fewer than 500 left in the wild. We left Bale National Park in a hired 4x4 truck with driver, picked up from our final campground location, and turned our attention to the other sights of the land.

Did you know that Ethiopia is seven years behind our calendar? Even though today is 10 December 2007, here in Ethiopia I believe today is 31 March 2000 – they celebrated their millennium in September, so three months ago. Anyway, yesterday, in a town called Awasa, we witnessed the 'Ethiopian Nations Nationalities and People's Day' at the

New Millennium Festival. It was a celebration of all the tribes, their language and culture, and the president was even present to make a speech. Because we were 'farangi' we were allowed in the VIP area, and were right beside the procession of tribes as they made their way to behind the stage.

We arrived at 9 am and, after several speeches and the parade of tribes, we watched as each tribe (there were 69 present) got a chance to perform on stage for 3–5 minutes. They chanted and sang and used instruments created from natural materials, like wood or horns. They were all unique, with different body paints and scars, clothing and hairdos, beads around different parts of the body, topless or wearing leopard skins, circular clay plates in their lips or bands of coiled metal around their neck ... absolutely incredible to witness. And Stu was at the front with all the reporters, taking picture after picture and bopping along to the music.

It was wonderful to witness these beautiful, dark-skinned women in Ethiopia, but shocking to hear the reason for their tradition of wearing large ceramic plates in their lower lips. We learned that lip plates were (and still are) considered important to drive away slave traders – women who have distorted the nature and size of their lips become less attractive, thereby decreasing their value as slaves. Incredible.

We left Awasa and drove west, with our mission to meet some of the local tribes of the land.

On the drive we watched as the countryside unfolded into a bright-green landscape, with beautiful lakes and hills, and dotted with wooden huts. We saw small African children running out to the roads; and African women, bent at the waist, carrying massive loads of wood, water, etc, on their backs; while the men remained unburdened, some with guns slung over their shoulders or lying under bushes for shade.

Today we went to an amazing local market, where three tribes converged to sell their wares. It was incredible to walk amongst these tribal people, whose lives are so radically different from our own. They are proud people – you can tell from the way they walk, and you should see how they decorate themselves. Beads laced throughout their hair, at least on the sides where it hadn't been shaven, along their foreheads, around their necks, around their arms, around their chest, waist, legs – everywhere! And they were wearing short sarongs or sheepskin shields around their middles. It was amazing. And you could see them looking at us – some with curiosity, some with indifference – as we were conspicuous foreigners. We took pictures of these people and paid them Br 2 ($0.20) per individual in the photo!

I learned that in the tribal village a man can have up to five wives (if he can afford it)! And you can tell the order of the wives by the position of the large metal ring around each of their necks. Their lives are very simple. Either they take care of livestock (goats and cattle), or they grow grains or potatoes to sell at the market. Very basic.

This first interaction with the native tribes was a positive experience. After staying here for the night, we looked forward to our next encounter, venturing off in our 4x4 to our next remote destination.

Today is Friday 14 December 2007. On the journey down yesterday, we drove on a dirt road in the middle of nowhere, where once in a while you would see tribal children, women or men walking along the barren road. The children would chase after our car screaming 'Highland!', the name of the company that produces water; in other words, they wanted water bottles. We handed out quite a few. At one point we stopped the car to take a picture of Stu beside a topless tribal woman, and within five minutes we were surrounded by 20–25 tribesmen armed with guns and machetes. They started to look into the car and, with the energy in the air starting to change, we quickly departed, relieved when we had gained some distance. When we finally reached Turmi, we could feel the difference compared with the last village.

Whereas the mood in the last village had been indifferent, open and friendly, this village was slightly hostile, begging and closed. From the minute we walked the dirt roads, we were followed by men and women, signalling that they wanted money and food from us; this was so different from the other tribes, where it was usually children begging and the elders showing respect. When we went for dinner we had rocks thrown at us and had to draw the curtains to protect ourselves. Crazy! Get me out of here!

We returned to our basic accommodation, locked the door and bunkered down for the night, overheating in our cell but, due to the hostility that surrounded us, not willing to open the entrance for ventilation. We were ready to leave at first light and were relieved as the village faded into the distance. We talked about the effects of the massive highways that were being constructed across the country by the Chinese, and how the tribes' worlds would change forever when the modern world entered their lives. We spent our last night together in a wonderfully modern hotel with hot showers, before parting ways with Dez and Lorena, as well as our car and our driver.

Adel, Tony, Stu and I now headed south for the border of Kenya, while Dez and Lorena returned to the capital, Addis Ababa.

15 December 2007. This morning we left our deluxe hotel, said goodbye to Dez and Lorena, and took a local bus to Moyale, a town on the border with Kenya. My goodness – what a difference from one side of the border to the other. Ethiopia had had paved roads, clean sidewalks and friendly people, whereas Kenya has dusty roads, dirty streets and a clearly machismo mentality. The men stared at Adel and me and, from some of the comments and winks, we could tell they thought that men were far superior to us weak, subordinate females. What losers!

Near the bus station we found very basic accommodation, with a central courtyard where a large group of men congregated, and bedrooms with metal bars in place of windows, for security purposes. We could feel the threatening, negative energy of the place, and Stuart remained on guard throughout the night, having barricaded us in our cell, and keeping his army knife within easy reach.

We woke up early after a horrible night's sleep, overheated and mosquito-bitten, hearing loud bangs and men yelling, and walked to the centre of town to catch our bus. We saw the bus waiting there and bought our tickets. Then, after watching for an hour as it was unloaded, we were told that the driver had decided that he wasn't going to leave today (Sunday) and maybe not tomorrow, and that we would have to take a truck. Oh no! We needed to get ourselves sorted quickly as it was essential to be amongst the armed military convoy heading south. So, for 500 shillings (exchange rate: Ksh 60h to US$1), we climbed on top of hundreds of bags of beans held within the walls of the large truck, and tried to get comfortable for the 700 km drive to the capital. At first we were pleased to have a military escort, with the extra security in an unsafe zone, but were surprised when the convoy sped off in the distance in front of us, and we eventually lost sight of it altogether. Then, about 20 minutes later, we were stopped by a military road block and we recognised the same individuals that had started the journey with us at the border. But this time they didn't look or act as friendly towards us. We all had to pull out our passports, and were shocked when one of our co-riders, a black man, was aggressively pulled from our vehicle and forced onto his knees, with a soldier screaming at him while shoving the butt of his gun against his head. Our driver was told to move on, and I will never forget the man's face as we left him, full of fear and panic. Terrifying.

Nine hours later, after a full day of travel, sitting on bags of beans along very hot and dusty roads, Tony and Adel decided that they had had enough and were going to get off at the next town and find a motel for the night. Stu and I would have preferred to continue the journey as the truck was bound for our end destination, the capital city of Nairobi, but we were reluctant to split the group and so got off at the same time. We found a hotel, had a shower, ate some food in the hotel's restaurant and then went to bed. Good night!

The following morning, Adel came out of her room puking, and my stomach was twisting and cramped. We needed to find a bus to take us to Isiolo, 309 km south, but 'no go'. No Buses. We were in the middle of no-man's land, a tiny pocket of civilisation that was unsafe due to the conflict in the surrounding area, a place that was scorched and roasting under the equatorial sun. We started to realise our predicament and regretted leaving our ride from the night before.

Stuart began roaming the streets, searching for transport for us, and finally found a truck going south. Great! Or not ...

The truck was loaded with 80–90 goats. There was only one seat available in the cab, which Adel needed as she was really unwell. So Tony, Stu and I climbed up the metal bars and sat in the only space available towards the back of the top of the truck. The bars needed to be in place in case the truck's load needed to be covered and protected, so ran from front to back and side to side. And we had to position ourselves on top of the bars, sitting above the goats. I didn't know whether I felt worse for the goats, packed in like sardines, with a worker having to go in and pull them to their feet to prevent from being squished to death, or for ourselves.

I have to say that, in all my years, I have NEVER had a worse day of travel in my life. When the truck proceeded down the dirt road and started gaining speed, the three of us literally had to hang on for our lives. Every bump flicked us up, flinging our legs up above our heads, and the only thing that kept us on the truck was our vice-like grip on the two bars. If the truck braked suddenly, we'd fly forwards. I was seriously scared. Not fun. Really *scary. After one hour we stopped in a small village, and I took the opportunity to move forward to be on top of the cab, which had been vacated for a few moments as its passengers stretched their legs – I could no longer handle being at the very back. My wrists felt like they were broken from hanging on so tightly and I was an emotional mess. This spot was better ... not great, but better. At 11 am we stopped for a lunch break and at this point my stomach turned for the worse. Great. Adel still wasn't feeling well, so she went in the cab, and I went back on top. About 20 minutes into the drive, I was sitting facing the back when I was smacked in the shoulders and head by the branch of a tree we passed. It HURT. This was not good. With my sunglasses on, I lowered my head and fought back tears as I was tossed around, hitting the bars with my ribs and back, hating every moment. By 1 pm, after 4.5 hours of riding on top, I nearly gave up hope, almost wishing that I would fall off, just to end the ride. I was bruised, bleeding, sore and depressed. But Tony had it worse: he was peeing blood, brought on by being thrown around in every direction and jarring his body in ways it wasn't meant to be. Great. I wish we had taken a flight. Lesson learnt.*

The ride finally came to an end and I swore I would never travel like that again in my life. We found a hotel and the following day boarded a bus bound for Nairobi, finally having paved roads under our tyres. We were going to stay in a proper house for the next ten days; my parents' best friend's brother worked for the Canadian consulate, and he had invited us to stay at his place while he returned to Canada for a two-week holiday. We felt like we had died and gone to heaven as we relaxed, cleaned and refreshed after our three days of travel, with a glass of wine and being served amazing Indian dishes by their Indian maid.

We organised a three-day tour in the famous Masai Mara Nature Reserve and were thrilled to encounter the 'Big Five' on our first day there, but were less than thrilled by the 'off-roading' that the tour vehicles exhibited in this one and only park. They hounded the animals by chasing them down, running the vehicles all over the terrain and into the bushes to get a better look at them, not giving them any peace. And there were so many vehicles all conglomerating around each animal that you were lucky if you could even glimpse the beast, rather than just the 20–30 vehicles stuffed with tourists. This was not the type of safari I was used to and, even though we did have many close encounters with lions and cheetahs, we knew this wasn't the type of animal encounter we'd choose in the future. And there was one scene that stood out from the rest.

We came to a stretch of river where, two weeks earlier, the wildebeest had crossed on their migration to the Serengeti. Millions of them had crossed, but there were casualties: close to 2,000 had died or been killed on the crossing, so the river was littered with carcasses. It STANK. There were Nile crocodiles on the banks, hippos in the water, and hundreds of vultures and marabou storks picking at the remains of the dead bodies. What a spectacle!

In the evening we sat around a fire, thrilled when ten Masai warriors came and joined us. We were entranced as they performed their traditional dance, jumping many feet into the air. Adel and I joined in when asked, leaping as high as we could, but were no match for these true athletes. We all enjoyed ourselves in the shadows of the dancing fire.

Our next plans were to head to Uganda to meet up with Adel's sister, Leyla, and her boyfriend and rafting guru, Pete.

3 January 2008. It's crazy how much stuff can happen in a week. We're in Uganda at the present and it's amazing how PLEASED this makes us. We left Nairobi on 28 December, the day after the national elections. Luckily, the counting of the ballots took a while so no results were released while we were still there. We found out after we crossed the border that ours was the last bus through and that the border closed soon after. Kenya is presently 'off limits' – violence and riots have kicked off big time, all due to the current president corrupting the votes and announcing that he had won (again). The opposition leader and tribes had a punch- up with him and his supporters, and 300 people have already been killed. We heard a sad story of where people in one village had sought refuge in a church, and a mob locked them in and burned them alive – at least 50 people were inside when the church went up in flames. On TV we can see looting and fighting, and tyres burning in the streets. We counted our blessings when we learned that the bus that left one hour after ours, a bus that we had been contemplating taking, was ambushed. Thank God we are here!

Uganda is much quieter than Kenya; the people are friendly and the environment is lush and beautiful. Pete and Leyla took us all rafting on New Year's Day and then we stayed on the Nile, at the place of one of their friends, celebrating long into the night with a great group of people. The rafting was awesome: 5+ rapids (the most extreme you can get), and we felt safe in Pete's hands, as he is one of the world's best. We are now in Kampala, the capital, trying to make our way to see the mountain gorillas, but it's not easy – Uganda has NO fuel. They usually get their fuel from Kenya, but since all borders are closed, this country is struggling; all prices have tripled or quadrupled. OMG!

We were headed to Bwindi Impenetrable Forest, a sanctuary inhabited by half the world's population of the critically endangered mountain gorillas – there are around 300 left in this forest. The sanctuary is bordered by the very dangerous Democratic Republic of Congo. I knew that Stuart had had an amazing encounter with the gorillas in 1995, when he journeyed on his own from Egypt to South Africa, making his way through Rwanda to visit the gorillas that Dian Fossey had studied and that had been the subject of the movie

Gorillas in the Mist. I couldn't wait to have my own story with these incredible primates.

We've done it! Today is Tuesday 8 January 2008, and we've seen the gorillas. It took Stuart the past four days of secret negotiating and meeting in strange locations, but he did it. He was able to get us in to the gorillas, even though it's been booked out for months. Yesterday we handed over US$250 each and walked up, up, up and over a mountain and down the other side – four hours of hiking – to find the endangered mountain gorilla. Since we didn't have the correct permits (which would have cost $500 each), we climbed in silence and often had to stop and sit in silence waiting for the 'official' group of eight to climb in front of us. We started at 9 am and were at the site where the gorillas were, by 1 pm, but had to wait another hour as the group in front had decided to have their packed lunches on the side of the hill. We had to be patient. But the time finally arrived and our guide motioned us to follow him ... to the gorillas. There were small babies, juveniles, three females and a giant male silverback. It was amazing to see them so close, only a few feet away from us! The silverback, with his huge gleaming chest, sat in the shade of some bushes, pulling branches towards himself, diligently pulling the bark off with his teeth. At first, the troop was out in the open, walking within five feet from where we stood. Then, after about ten minutes, they moved further into the bushes, seeking shade. It was an unbelievable experience to witness their interactions and their mannerisms, and we all stood there transfixed, in awe of these beautiful creatures.

After 40 minutes of viewing, our guide told us we had to go as he didn't want the 'anti-poaching unit' to find us there. We were just starting to move away when we heard the sound of a firearm being cocked. Oh my

God! They have a shoot-to-kill policy here, as poaching is a massive problem for this endangered animal, and we knew we were in trouble when our guide gave us hand signals to run. We stampeded like elephants through the bush, making so much noise that anyone – let alone an experienced tracker – could find us. I was shocked to see Tony sprint past Adel, disappearing into the forest – I don't think I'd ever seen him run before! Two of the three guides also disappeared and my panic rose as we fled for our lives. We were then given the signal to get down, and the next minute were lying flat on the ground, trying to camouflage ourselves on the forest floor.

I was lying there with Adel beside me, scared shitless, thinking 'this is it', that this was the way my life would end. I could hear screaming, and out of the corner of my eye watched our black guide looking terrified as he moved towards the two gunmen, his hands in the air, obviously explaining our position and begging for his life. The new arrivals were upset, yelling at our guide and pointing their guns at his head, forcing him onto his knees, with his hands on his head.

It was at this point that Stuart jumped up, making his presence known and shouting 'Mzungu, mzungu!' The guns swivelled in Stuart's direction and I held my breath, not knowing what their next move would be. We could be killed or put in an African jail – equally terrifying prospects. The men's eyes were bloodshot red, as if they were on drugs or hadn't slept in days, and I prayed like there was no tomorrow, hoping that they would let us go peacefully. Adel and I sat up at this point, and with three *mzungu* (Swahili for white person) in their midst, the gunmen focused again on our guide and a lengthy conversation ensued. Ten minutes later, our guide came to us and informed us that we needed to pay these guys off; we handed over all the money we had on us, 60,000 Ugandan shillings. We were off the hook. We breathed a huge sigh of relief and hightailed it out of there.

The gorilla experience tested our fear. We had also been warned about the outbreak of Ebola in south-western Uganda, where we now were. Next, we were told about the unrest in neighbouring Congo and how 800,000 people were running for their lives since the tribes were murdering and raping anyone in their path. And lastly how some tourists had been killed in 1999, in the camp that we were staying in, by men from the Congo. Jesus. Africa can be a hard place.

Before leaving our camp we took a one-day walking tour of the surrounding area. We spent some time with a local witch doctor, who showed us a variety of healing plants from the surrounding forest. And we visited a Pygmy village, where Adel and I danced with the men and boys, towering over the individuals known for their short stature.

We returned by bus to Jinja and stayed again with Adel's sister, Leyla. In the days that followed, Stu and I went river rafting on the Nile, spending whole days on the water, tackling some massive water and nerve-racking waterways. We rented a vehicle, taking Leyla with us as we visited Sipi Falls for a few nights away. Then the four of us were off, bound for a ten-day adventure, with the first stop being Murchison Falls National Park. As luck would have it, Stu bumped into an Aussie at a Shell petrol station and, after we learnt that he worked at a Jane Goodall chimp project, our plans changed. We joined him as he returned to home base, staying the night in the newly built dorm and planning a 'chimp walk' for the next morning.

Our guide was Justin, a nine-year veteran of the park area, who studied the animals from 8 am to 5 pm most days; we were in experienced hands. We could hear the chimps within ten minutes of walking and found them soon after. We watched as they travelled through the forest, swinging effortlessly from branch to branch, moving swiftly through the foliage above our heads.

Along one of the trails, we found a two-month-old colobus monkey lying on the ground, looking as if it had been dropped from above and showing very little energy. Stu told us about how this was probably the result of a monkey hunt, where chimps would group together and hunt other monkeys, and where sometimes a mother would drop its young at the last minute in order to escape being caught herself. Stu doctored the monkey and brought him back to base, with the hope that he would get healthy and thrive, being looked after there by the staff. It was amazing to cuddle something so small, and gosh, he was so cute.

After the walk we said our goodbyes and headed to Murchison Falls, where the Nile River funnels through a 7-metre gap and falls 43 metres through a channel. The sound, vibrations and energy of the place were amazing! Spectacular nature.

We continued our tour and went on a number of game drives, taking hundreds of photos of the local elephants, Cape buffalos, giraffes, hyenas, lions and the huge variety of birds. The following day we went on a water tour, coming close to hippos and Nile crocodiles, and drifting close to the pounding torrential water at the base of the funnelled channel. It was outstanding. Next we headed for the famous Queen Elizabeth Park, in the western region of Uganda.

We stayed five nights in this park, driving our Corolla vehicle along the dirt roads, wishing we had opted for the recommended 4x4 – the tracks were littered with massive potholes, some as large as our car. But it was all worth it. We saw so many animals and the landscape was out of this world, some parts with incredible craters filled with flamingos and beautiful lakes. We stayed most nights in an open-area campground and had to light fires to keep the lions and hyenas at bay, having heard their nearby roars and cackling in the not-too-distant brush.

Last night, while we were in our tents, we had hippos come to within metres of us, so close that we could hear them chomping on the grass. I wasn't even allowed to go outside the tent to pee, instead having to position myself carefully in the outside enclosed area of the tent.

It was in this park that Tony and Stu were charged when they got too close to a hippo, and we all saw a wild aardvark for the first time in our lives and enjoyed so many other wild encounters. We often had to stop the car when a group of elephants blocked our path, and at one point we realised we were in a dangerous predicament as these massive tusked mammals travelled both in front of and behind our vehicle, blocking all escape paths. But all ended well and we left the park elated, having seen so much African wildlife.

After a last night together, we parted ways. Tony and Adel drove back to Jinja to stay with Leyla and to return our rental car, while Stuart and I flew to Zanzibar, Tanzania. We stayed for a few days in the historic Stone Town, a place made famous by its role within the slave trade.

We visited the old 'slave market' where slaves had been shoved into 10 ft × 10 ft rooms, 50 men in one room and 75 women and children in another. There were tiny slits, only a couple of inches wide, in the rock walls for ventilation, and we learned how many slaves had died of suffocation or starvation as they were held in these cellars, waiting for their lives to be sold. The story goes that the men were brought out, one by one, then tied to a massive tree – the 'Whipping Tree' – and flogged. The longer they were whipped without crying out, the higher the price on their head. Barbaric! And the babies and children were taken away from their mothers, often given as a bonus when a strong male slave was sold, or otherwise mercilessly slaughtered. Disgusting and heart-wrenching. Historically the slave trade operated from the 15th to the 19th century, officially ending in 1873, when it was written into law that it was no longer legal. Unfortunately slavery will never die as individuals value making money over life itself.

Our moods lightened as we travelled to the northern tip of the island. Here we found a great place to stay for the next two weeks, surrounded by wonderful people and great food.

One of the highlights here was the Lighthouse Aquarium, with its natural lagoon beside the ocean. The sea water in the lagoon would rise and fall as the tide came and went. Around the perimeter of the lagoon was an 8–10 ft natural wall, and inside was a lagoon about 30–40 ft across by 80 ft long. In the water were tons of fish (groupers, jacks, batfish, etc), and green and hawksbill turtles! The turtles were being looked after, fed and nursed until they were big enough to be released back into the wild. Supposedly the young hatchlings were gathered from their nests in the sand and brought here to be reared, and had a higher chance of survival than if they had been left to their own devices.

Stu and I paid an additional $5 each to get in the water ... and it was amazing. One of the workers would throw in seagrass and the turtles would clamber over to eat it, pushing us to the side with their flippers, eating within centimetres of our masked faces. We were able to touch their shells and flippers, and it was truly an amazing experience.

We left the island and returned to the capital, Dar es Salaam, where we met up with Tony and Adel to plan our next adventure, heading north to the Serengeti and Ngorongoro Crater. Stu and I took the nine-hour express bus to Arusha, the town where all the tours departed from, and spent the following day pounding the pavement, interviewing a number of tour agencies until we found one that met our requirements. Adel and Tony arrived with their British friend, Claire (who had flown in the previous day) and, after spending the night in the city, we set off on our five-day tour.

Our first stop brought us to Lake Manyara National Park, where we were thrilled to see loads and loads of elephants, some only metres away from our van, as well as hippos and Cape buffalos. But the highlight was the tree-climbing lions. There are only two populations in the whole world of such lions, which actually climb trees as part of their day-to-day behaviour. We were lucky enough to see two of the lions, one of which was only metres away from us. We returned to our camp, ate a delicious meal and retired to our tents in utter contentment.

The next day brought us to the world famous Serengeti, where we passed thousands of wildebeest and zebras, the remnants of the great migration, in which approximately four million animals journey from Kenya's Masai Mara Park to Tanzania's Serengeti Park. We enjoyed close-up sightings of lions and cheetahs and saw the usual contingent of giraffes and elephants, but it was only due to Stuart's keen animal observation that we had VIP seats for an actual kill, right in front of our eyes.

Along the side of the road, Stuart spotted a cheetah and asked our driver and guide, Edgar, to stop so we could watch it. Edgar, who had seemed reluctant to comply with any of our requests, kept moving forward, until Stuart put his foot down and ordered him to 'STOP!' You could tell Edgar was pissed off by his instruction, but what we were about to witness (and only Stu had seen the clues) was a cheetah stalk and kill! Oh my goodness. We watched as the cheetah rose from its reclining position, intent on its prey about 900 metres ahead. Then, as Stu asked Edgar to drive slowly forward, we saw a mother and baby gazelle on their own. Again, Stuart had to raise his voice to get Edgar to stop, and it was lucky that he did ... from our 'grandstand seats' we watched as the gazelles and cheetah played cat and mouse ... when the gazelle stopped, the cheetah stopped, and when the gazelle ran forward, the cheetah ran forward, quickly closing the gap. And a few minutes later it happened. About 15 metres from where we were stationed, the cheetah raced forward and targeted the infant, using its front paw to cause it to stumble, and finally catching its dinner. Incredible!

We spent the rest of the day on a high, enjoying the sights of the vast Serengeti National Park, and looking forward to the next day's activity, a visit to the famous Ngorongoro Crater. Known as one of the greatest natural wonders of this planet, as well as being the world's largest caldera, this area has wildlife coexisting with semi-nomadic Masai pastoralists, who practise traditional livestock grazing. And it is while we waited at the gates to the crater that we were surrounded by Masai warriors, who tried to sell us jewellery and even an authentic spear. Tony immediately started bargaining with them, buying the very sharp, double-ended spear for 20,000 shillings – a very cheap purchase that left him smiling for the rest of the trip.

Once inside the crater we viewed loads of animals: flamingos on the lake, hippos making funny noises, hyenas, jackals, elephants, zebras and a highly endangered black rhino with its calf. It was a fantastic day, and we knew we were seeing the best that nature had to offer.

We enjoyed one last game safari before heading back to Arusha, and after dumping our bags off at the hotel and cleaning ourselves off, we all went out for a lovely meal, toasting our successes in the parks. This would be our last night together as a group, since Stuart and I still had one more country to visit: the island of Madagascar. We went over the highlights of our past four months together, and smiled at the fact that our relationship was as strong as ever. Goodbye friends and hello new adventures.

We had a number of concerns as our shuttle drove us back to the border of Kenya. First, I had seen on the morning news the headline: 'Cyclone Ivan Hits Madagascar' – a grade-five hurricane was hammering the capital, Antananarivo, the city we were flying in to. But the main concern was that Kenya was still in turmoil following the December presidential elections, with more than 1,000 people killed and 300,000 displaced due to tribal genocide. And right now we were driving into Kenya, headed for Nairobi's international airport.

Stuart decided that it would be safer to stay the night at the airport, rather than venturing into the city at night, and was able to persuade one of the workers in the departure area to let us pass through customs and into the departure lounge, removing ourselves from the over-crowded mezzanine area. With our backpacks on, we headed for the 'sleeping lounge', looking for a room to rest our weary heads, only to find they were completely full. Now what?

'Let's put up out tent,' Stuart says.

'In an airport?' I reply.

'Why not?' replies Stu.

So that is what we did.

After a night interrupted by loud announcements screaming from the speakers, we packed up the tent and went for breakfast, watching CNN's announcements on cyclone Ivan's devastating path across Madagascar. Help us, Lord. Do we go or don't we? Are we risking our lives flying into a cyclone? After talking to an Air Madagascar representative and confirming the flight was safe – the cyclone had already passed the region we would be flying into – we decided to stick to our plan and go for it. And we were so thankful we did.

We were guided to stay in Haute Ville ('higher town') by a fellow passenger, who had befriended us on the plane when she came over to ask how we had managed to get through security with our backpacks and tents. She became our guardian angel in Madagascar, advising us on places to stay and see. She took us in her hired taxi and dropped us off at the Hotel Le Jean Laborde, a lovely residence rich in history and surrounded by cobblestone streets and European buildings.

Once settled, we left our hotel and ventured out on foot, passing the superb palace and lake, surprised by the number of 'tea houses' dotted around the city, and by the fact that we had to buy rain jackets – the weather was still unsettled after the cyclone. The features of the people there were quite different from those we had seen on the continent, having a more Indonesian/Malaysian look to them. They had been influenced by the British and, more recently, by French rule, which was clearly evident from the large number of croissants and baguettes available, as well as with French being the second main language spoken, after Malagasy.

We organised a flight to Fort Dolphin on the south of the island, where our friends Daniel and Chen lived. They had worked beside us at Bamboozi Resort in Tofo, Mozambique, and had invited us to come and visit. Daniel and Chen spoiled us, touring us around the area with guitars and surfboards in hand, taking us to beaches and providing us with home-cooked meals. But the highlight was our visit to the Lemur Reserve.

Within minutes of entering, we had three Verreaux's sifakas (white lemurs) come down from the high branches and eat bananas from our hands. They were so gentle and would place their hands, which had very soft padding, on our hands as they ate. So gentle, calm and cute. Then ten minutes later we looked behind us, and in came a squadron of ring-tailed lemurs. These guys were much more active, actually jumping on us and sitting on our shoulders, grabbing the bananas and demolishing them within seconds.

It was an amazing day and we spent hours here, resting under the branches and watching as the white lemurs hopped across the lawn in front of us, with arms held straight up in the air and their hind legs propelling them sideways. A fascinating sight to behold.

Before leaving, Daniel took us to the 'environmental area' of the mining operation where he worked, where they were carrying out research on the indigenous flora and fauna, trying to compile as much information (on life cycles, pollinating insects, preferences to sun/shade, etc) on the endemic species before it was too late and species were lost forever. Less than 10 per cent of primary forest was left on the island, and there was very little information on which species were still present. We learned that about 90 per cent (!!) of all plant and animal species found in Madagascar are endemic, i.e. found nowhere else in the world, and that this distinctive ecology was being quickly erased due to human interference. Not a pretty tale. Before leaving the site, we got to see a rare and endangered fosa, the only predator of the lemur, which looks like a mix between a dog and a cat, with its dog-snout face, a cat-like body, a long tail, and claws for climbing trees. A unique animal.

We left our friends after a day's hike up a mountain, capturing amazing views of the coast of this easterly region. Then we flew to Toliara on the west coast, a place known for its diving and beautiful coastline. We went out on a two-dive day package, but due to the heavy rains of the cyclone, coupled with the extensive logging in the area, the water was filled with silt. Visibility was incredibly poor and we abandoned our idea of further dives, continuing instead on our journey.

We took a 'taxi-brousse' (a local minibus) to our next destination, Ranohira, watching as we sped past baobab trees, with their distinctive swollen stems. We had planned a two-day hike in the Park National de L'Isalo from Ranohira and were guided the following morning past rice fields to the base of a canyon. This is where our guide left us. We found lemurs jumping from tree to tree, and then began the arduous climb up the mountain, rewarded with stunning views when we reached the top. We were amazed by the layered sandstone pinnacles of terracotta rock, awestruck by the stunning vista of rock formations, and we walked along the sandy path for 14 kilometres until we came to a beautiful waterfall and pool, close to our campsite. Stuart and I were sweaty and dusty from our hike under the hot sun and quickly jumped into the cool refreshing water, reenergising our souls. Our tent site had wild lemurs all around, and we laughed as we watched them vying for the best spots and hanging upside down on the branches, trying to steal our food.

The following day we trekked to stunning natural pools within a canyon area, where Stu jumped in for a dip, and then we hiked for several hours, ending our tour with a great sense of accomplishment. We caught the next bus out of town, squashed into our seats as the vehicle was stuffed beyond its capacity. We endured a very uncomfortable journey, moving from one crammed bus to another and crossing more than 700 kilometres to return to the capital. With time against us and still so much to see, we had made the decision to visit one last park, famous for its indri population, and took one last bus north to the Park National d'Andasibe.

We were delighted to wake up, in our A-frame accommodation, to the magical calls of the indri. We were situated on a hill opposite the park and were able to spot two with our binoculars. It didn't take us long before we found a guide and booked ourselves in for a forest walk.

We were really lucky as we got to see woolly lemurs, which are nocturnal creatures, within the first 20 minutes of our walk. And then we came across three indris!! So cool. They look like warped panda bears, with black and white markings, teddy-bear faces and elongated legs. We spent about 30 minutes with them, following them into the forest, past vines, branches and trees, watching as they jumped (up to ten metres!) from tree to tree. Eventually they came closer and closer, moving down the trunks, and – the highlight – they started to call out, and we listened to their high-pitched wails from just three metres away.

The indris' vocalisations are the loudest in the animal kingdom, ringing out for short bursts of four to five minutes each, so we'd always stop and listen to the sound whenever we heard them. We were impressed by the lemurs of the forest, but also had close encounters with chameleons as well as with a leaf gecko, an endemic species that blends into the tree bark superbly – an impressive feat of nature. Stuart had been on the look-out for a leaf gecko since the start of our trip. To help him get a better look at this camouflaged creature, which was just out of reach, I went down onto my hands and knees so Stu could stand on my back and get some great photos.

Our week passed quickly, but not without mishap: Stuart banged his head into a jagged edge of a wooden frame, cutting a gash into his skull ...

I'm in the shower when I hear a bang, and a few moments later I hear Stuart calling me to come out of the shower to go to him, but for me not to panic. What the heck?! Wrapped in a towel, I rush outside to see Stu with blood all over his face, in his hair, dripping onto his shirt and pants. JESUS CHRIST! He asks me to check the cut to see the severity of it (to gauge whether he'll bleed to death!) and at first I can't even see it because of all the blood. After a few seconds of investigation I see the gash, about 4 cm long and 3 mm wide. He needs stitches. So I run back to our original room, the room from which we had just moved, then back again to pack our stuff and move rooms ... in such a panic and daze, not knowing what I should do. At first, Stu thinks I can mend the cut with the surgical tape we have, but the tape doesn't stick to his hair and scalp, so we need another option. Luckily, one of the workers comes to tell us there's a doctor nearby and a car waiting for us. With great relief, we grab our money belts and coats, and go.

The doctor starts by cutting Stu's hair away from the cut, much to his chagrin, then proceeds to put in two stitches with a two-inch, curved needle, which is very blunt. It looks really painful as Stu sits there with his head being pulled and pinned by the unsharpened needle, OUCH! But he sits silently while he is pushed and prodded, and is relieved when it's done. All for 10,000 ariary – about US$5.50 – not bad.

With a lot less blood but with full memory cards on our cameras, we returned to the capital and spent our last days just being tourists.

As I look back at our time in Madagascar, I think first of hillsides with valleys filled with rice fields. Rice fields were everywhere, in any flat-lying area, sometimes creeping up the sides of mountains. There were few trees to be seen apart from inside the national parks, and the river and streams that we passed were a deep-orange colour, obviously due to soil that had been loosened by deforestation and then picked up by the moving water. The small villages that we passed often had two-storey homes built of red brick, with tiny shops occupying the ground floor. Many citizens wore ripped and stained clothes and walked barefoot along the roads, continually moving to the side as the blaring horns of the mini-vans and trucks warned them of their presence. Honking here is what they do best – you can hear the blasting sound at any time of the day.

Madagascar was a terrific way to end our African trip. We loved this country as it stood apart from the rest, home to stunning mountains, spectacular rainforests and beautiful white beaches. But the highlight had to be our close encounters with the lemurs, especially the indri. Their vocal calls will be a melody that remains lodged in my memory for the rest of my days.

Chapter 14
A New Direction in Life

'Your dad has had a stroke and is in the hospital.' My world dropped from underneath me as I stood there in a towel, dripping wet, having just been summoned out of the shower for this important phone call. I was speechless. My worst fear was coming true: something horrible had happened to a family member and I was on the other side of the world, now feeling completely helpless and utterly devastated. My mum described the events leading up to the event, the fact that my dad had been trying to fix a community swimming pool, standing hip-deep in freezing water for at least 30 minutes, then shortly after returning home he had had the stroke and been taken to the hospital. I wanted to be home, back in the circle of my family, and the tears would not stop as my mum tried to console me, saying that they wouldn't be clear on the severity of the stroke until after his brain scan. I felt absolutely useless as I hung up the phone, hanging on to Stu for dear life and breaking into uncontrollable sobs as my heart broke.

In the days that followed, I received updates on Dad's condition, being told that he was one of the lucky ones – the stroke had not left him paralysed in the face or anywhere else in the body, and he was comfortable in his solitary hospital room. It gave me some relief when I was finally able to talk to him directly, hearing him describe in his own words all that had happened before and after the event, and I was surprised by his upbeat and joking attitude. Dad reassured me that he was fine and that it was pointless for me to rush home to stand by his bedside, as he was being released from the hospital in a few days. He told me to finish my teaching contract first, then to come over in my usual time during the summer holidays, when he would be waiting for me with bells on.

The weeks dragged by and I was frightened every time the phone rang, scared that I would receive a call saying things had got worse and that my dad wouldn't be there when I arrived home in the summer. But luck was on our side – Dad's health didn't decline, and the only residual effect of the stroke was pain radiating down his leg and arm.

I returned to Vancouver, heading straight to Bowen Island to see my dad, and remaining beside him for several days. I was relieved to see that that he looked and sounded the same, but I could sense a change in him; Dad was acting more fatalistic and his body was in constant pain. He was easily frustrated when one of the family members took over a role that he used to fill – carrying or lifting objects, for example, was out of the question. I'd see him storm off in anger and stay in his bedroom, no doubt feeling restricted and worthless whenever one of us took over a job he was attempting to do.

Amber and Ali came up with a plan for the three of us to go to the inauguration of the Pemberton Festival. This was to be a three-day summer music festival, held in the picturesque setting at the foot of Mount Currie and the surrounding mountain range. Amber arranged a place for us to pitch our tents, staying in the backyard of some family friends in the area and, with a new focus, I counted the days until we would be together in this magical setting.

A New Direction in Life

We packed a number of different dancing outfits and sorted ourselves out in terms of supplies, knowing that this event would be epic; the main acts included Coldplay, Jay-Z, Tom Petty and the Heartbreakers, Nine Inch Nails, Tragically Hip and the Flaming Lips. We would be joined by my cousin, James, and his girlfriend, as well as a number of Amber's good friends and relatives, together creating an amazing dance group, all moving with massive grins on our faces to the rhythms that permeated the air. The best part was that Amber's sister, Tahlia, had a stall at the event, so had a small campervan in the nearby camping area. There we could stash our stuff and regroup, drinking various spirits as we reclined on her bed, deciding which performance we wanted to see. One night we skipped the stage acts to visit the dance tent, then pulsed to the beat that radiated through the speakers and through our feet, feeling free and at peace as we enjoyed our time together and our close connection. When the event was over it took us a couple of days to recuperate, but we smiled at the memories we'd created, loving our closeness and our crazy ways.

I was now 35 years old. In the back of my mind I had always thought that that would be the age at which I'd have to make a decision about having children. For so many years I had resisted the idea, not wanting to jeopardise my wonderful lifestyle, never wanting to go back to a standard working life with no real travel time. But I was now starting to reconsider, especially as our good friends Marci and Blue had had their first child, a little boy called Sonny, while I danced at the Pemberton Festival.

Could we bring a child into the world and drag him or her around with us wherever we went, or would having a child force us to change everything? When our lives felt so ideal, did we really want to change what we had by bringing another person into the equation?

I returned to the UK, hundreds of questions bubbling around in my head, and unloaded on Stuart. Did we want to have a child? Our friends had started to give us their opinions, thinking we were crazy to leave it so late, with some saying it had taken them two to four years before their children came to them, warning us about the high chances of miscarriage and the difficulties of conceiving. Really? I'd had NO idea. So, after some serious discussions, Stuart and I decided to pull the goalie and see what Mother Nature had intended, becoming more aware of my menstrual cycle and what the different phases meant in terms of productivity.

One day, knowing that I was ovulating, I called Stu to say that, if he wanted a child, he should return from his show rather than driving on to a new showground. And this is what he did. It felt weird, knowing that we were having sex with the purpose of creating a child, and it put a whole new perspective on the act, sharing our connection in reverence. And as fate would have it, I became pregnant on that first attempt. We were completely shocked when we were told by the nurse that our test was positive, and that we would be having a child in the next nine months. Oh my goodness!!

It's one thing to think you may have a child, but something completely different when you know you have one growing inside you. Our decision was now beyond recall, and we had to come to terms with the fact that we would be parents and no longer free, independent spirits that could venture off into the unknown without a care in the world. I had a beautiful step-daughter in Marie, but it was one thing to love a child that was growing up in another home and country, and quite another to have a baby under the same roof. The dawning realisation that my life had now changed forever sometimes made me burst into tears – I wasn't sure how this new being could fit into our lives, and I wrote intention lists, affirming how I wanted to see everything working out. Stuart and I agreed to tell everyone when we reached week 12 of the pregnancy, so, with the massive secret under our belts, we started our six-month holiday.

After a quick visit to Germany to visit Marie, we headed to France, where we had arranged a two-week holiday with my mum and dad. We stayed at a campground about 30 minutes outside Paris for the first few days, briefly joining Uncle Guy, who was just ending his own annual two-month holiday in his luxury campervan. Once he and his wife departed, our touring holiday began, with Stuart as our driver, my dad as co-pilot, and me and my mum in the back of the car.

We walked the streets of Paris, exploring the famous Louvre Museum and its amazing collection of ancient artefacts, passing the Champs-Élysées and the Arc de Triomphe, and taking in the magnificent Notre-Dame Cathedral. My mum and I dared each other to go to the top of the Eiffel Tower, so, leaving our husbands at ground level, we took the elevators to the top deck and were rewarded with amazing panoramic views of the capital. All the while, in the back of my mind, I wanted to tell my parents my secret, especially when we enjoyed such special moments in these unique settings. But I held my tongue, knowing they would be devastated if I miscarried before the arrival of their grandchild. We had convinced everyone that we were not going to have kids, so this announcement was going to shock a lot of people.

We drove out of Paris, stopping at a number of châteaux in the Loire Valley, completely awed by the grandeur and the opulence of some of the buildings there. We covered many miles, heading west and then north to the coast. We stopped at Mont Saint-Michel, a remarkable mediaeval, walled city, crowned by a great Gothic abbey that stands on a small granite outcrop, surrounded by an estuary and tidal waters. We visited the most popular town in Brittany, Saint-Malo, and walked the coastal boardwalk, surprised by my father's newfound fitness as he passed us, thankful for his days at the gym and his new lease on life. We rested in the many cafés, eating delectable meals, with Stuart secretly drinking my wine. One evening, as we sat at our restaurant table overlooking the sea, my dad raised a toast in our honour, admitting that he had been mistaken when he gave us a five-year time limit just before our wedding, and saying that he was very impressed by what the two of us had accomplished together.

We continued our tour, seeking out one of the World War II cemeteries, searching for the tombstone of my grandmother's brother. He had died at the age of 22, only a month before the war ended. We found his grave beside thousands of others – all young soldiers who had died fighting for their country – and our hearts dropped as we realised that the most common age of death was between 18 and 25 years old. Incredibly sad. We finished our time in Versailles, visiting the royal palace, where we were blown away by the Hall of Mirrors, the Grand Apartments and the royal gardens. The sheer opulence of each room was outstanding and we could understand why the citizens had revolted in the French Revolution – the monarchy had hoarded everything while the citizens starved to death.

We left France and flew to Vancouver, enjoying a low-key visit to my parents' place on Bowen Island. Stuart and I organised a family dinner towards the end of the month, where we formally announced our new addition. Everyone was thrilled by the news, toasting the health of the baby, and as we sat there surrounded by family, we knew we had made the right decision. It was at this time that I found out that Sarah, my best friend and neighbour at Pasley, was also pregnant; it was great to be able to share my pregnancy experience with a girlfriend who was going through the same changes.

Our next port of call was New Zealand. We had decided to wait until Christmas to broadcast the news to Stuart's family, but suspicions grew as I didn't imbibe my usual number of alcoholic drinks with my sisters-in-law, and my brother-in-law noticed that my stomach was expanding. Everyone was ecstatic when we told them we were expecting, and they made us promise to return next year to introduce the new baby to all the cousins.

Stuart and I travelled to our property in the south and stayed in a friend's caravan while we spent two days in our garden, ripping out whole sections of overgrowth, taming the wild appearance of the area. The neighbourhood was improving in looks and, even though we'd only owned this property for a year, we thought of selling it and making a profit.

After a quick visit to my adopted New Zealand family in Blenheim, we packed our bags and headed to Australia, travelling to visit Stuart's uncle, Rob. My stomach was growing and I was feeling great. I was one of the lucky ones who didn't get morning sickness or any of the other negative symptoms due to pregnancy, and I felt wonderful as I walked the white sands of the beaches of Greens Pool Reserve. The days on Rob's farm passed quickly, and before I knew it, I was returning to England on my own, having secured a teaching position in a nearby school while Stuart went on his boys' trip to China and Mongolia.

I had never been in the UK in late February before and it didn't take me long to promise myself that I wouldn't be doing it again. The wind was always howling in Norfolk, transporting a freezing breeze, chilling me to the bone as it entered our old mobile home through the many holes scattered on its shell. I soon regretted my early return. The weeks passed and the weather eventually brightened, and then Stuart returned. But within a week of his return we had a new visitor in our midst – Stuart's eldest brother, Garry, had flown in, with no money in his wallet and no place to go.

Chapter 15
A Real Life-changer

'Stuart! Mum's driving me to the hospital. The baby's coming!' I could tell that my announcement had been broadcast to an audience at the Royal Bath & West Showground, where my husband was performing his show, since the response to my revelation was a massive roaring of shrieks and applause. Stuart had kept the phone on his person as he walked onto the stage – something he'd never done before in his life, but after my call earlier in the day, telling him about the waves of pain, he had known that something was up. Now he immediately jumped off the stage, ran to his car and drove like a bat out of hell to try and make it to the delivery room in time.

I had finished my teaching position four days earlier and my mum had flown in a day after that, ready to help me out. Stuart's schedule was completely booked and he would be away on shows most of the time on and around the baby's due date. We were as ready as we could be, having purchased a small caravan that we placed next door to our mobile home for my mum to sleep in, as well as creating a baby's room by adding an extra wall inside our place. We felt we were ready for our simple lives to change forever, with the addition of Baby Barnes. We were happy, healthy and excited, and looked forward to extending our family by one.

I won't go into too many details about the birth, except to say that our baby was in the wrong position, with its back against my own, which caused me excruciating pain. I was ready for the 'severe period pains'

I had been forewarned about, but this pain in my back felt like someone was holding a knife inside my spine. I asked for an epidural injection; after an hour, an anaesthetist finally came to perform this delicate spinal procedure, but it was too late. The drugs had no effect on the pain as the baby was coming too quickly. In less than two and a half hours, from start to finish, a little baby girl was born, and I welcomed Eva into our family, pleased when she immediately latched on to feed.

Stuart arrived within 30 minutes of the birth, frustrated that he had been caught in traffic jams and not made it in time to be present for the arrival of his child. But we focused on the present and how fortunate we were to have a healthy child. Once all the hospital checks and forms had been completed, we all went home – I didn't want to remain in a ward with seven other woman with screaming babies all around, even though it was only six hours since I had given birth. At home we all fell exhausted into bed, asleep within minutes and not waking up for eight hours. Eva also slept for this amount of time, and I thought I must be one of the lucky ones with an 'easy baby', but I was in for a rude awakening.

After my mum left, I felt like my life was on 'survival mode' – I was not enjoying my existence. Nobody had told me that I would be ripped and torn during the birth, that I would bleed heavily for weeks after the delivery, that my nipples would be in excruciating pain while the baby began to nurse, or that I would be so sleep-deprived that it was all I could do to change out of my pyjamas at the start of the day. Everyone had said I'd feel this immediate attachment and unconditional love for my baby, and I felt even worse for not feeling this connection. But the main problem was that my child had 'colic' –

the undefined term that they give to any unsettled child – and Eva would scream and bend backwards in pain every time I fed her, which in the beginning was every couple of hours, all day and all night long. Her screams would tear into me; they were high-pitched wails that would last for hours, and there were times when I'd have to put her down and walk away, bawling my eyes out because I felt like I wanted to shake her to make her shut up.

Stuart was away working, the majority of my friends were either in Devon or Canada, and I felt I struggled from day to day. When Stuart did come back from work, he took over and would try his hardest to give me a break, doing the night shifts and taking Eva away with him when he was on the farm. I could sense that he had a strong connection with our little girl and I'd try not compare myself with him, but the weeks had taken their toll; my energy was at an all-time low. Marie and her mum, Kirsten, came over for a week and I tried to give the impression that everything was alright. But on the inside I felt like I was withering away, completely exhausted both day and night. Wendy came to see me a couple of times, but she and Duncan now had two little girls of their own, two-year-old Miki and nine-month-old Eleni. Stuart would also call our mutual friend, Marigold, to come over, especially when I'd phone him while he was at a show, holding the phone to a crying Eva and telling him that I wasn't coping well. And then there was my dad, who continually told me on Skype that I was suffering from postnatal depression and that I should go and talk to my doctor.

After six weeks of hell, I returned to Canada for a summer visit, hoping to get some help from my family, and was completely unprepared for all the events that were happening at the time – there seemed to be so many negative and disheartening things happening. First there was the death of my older sister's best friend, who had been in her early 40s and who left behind two beautiful young boys and a broken husband. My older sister and my dad had just bought Labradoodle puppies, then unfortunately my sister's dog became sick, leading to a $2,000 vet bill, money that was needed in other areas of life. And during those few weeks in Canada I found out that one of my cousins was forced to have an emergency caesarean after discovering that she had cancer behind her eye, which needed to be operated on as soon as possible. She delivered a healthy baby girl, but could not see her due to her recent blindness, and could not breastfeed her due to the drugs they were giving her for the cancer. A terrible predicament to be in. These were only a few of the terrible events taking place during this time, and it was the first time in my life that I felt almost relieved to be leaving Canada to return to the UK. I recognised that this was a major turning point for me as I left my self-focused world and started to regain my moral strength and focus, comparing myself with others and seeing again how truly lucky I was.

On my return I found out that we had sold our South Island New Zealand property, securing ourselves a good profit in our one-year investment, and that we finally had money in the bank. And I focused my attention on our next six-month holiday, looking for destinations close to New Zealand or Australia, where we could go for a month in between the family visits. After a lot of research I finally settled on New Caledonia, the French-speaking island off Australia's east coast, which has one of the largest lagoons in the world and is surrounded by the New Caledonia Barrier Reef. One of the main incentives for this location was the fact that I had found an unbelievable deal on the internet, a car rental for just £150 per week. I reserved the vehicle after contacting the head office to confirm the price, but had to do this in four separate individual weekly bookings as they wouldn't allow me to book it in a single one-month time frame. But since New Caledonia was an incredibly expensive destination, I didn't mind the paperwork, and printed off our reservation to put with the rest of the documents for our travels. Our travel plans were set and we were soon leaving the UK, saying farewell to our newfound friends, Naomi and Matt – a lovely British lady and her Kiwi husband – who made great efforts to be helpful and supportive, securing our friendship for life.

Our travel routine had been drastically altered by our family addition – our two backpacks would now be accompanied by a stroller, car seat, large suitcase and changing bag. Our years of travelling light were behind us and we now felt like Sherpas, struggling to find the space and the strength to transport our baby and all the necessary baggage. We took turns looking after Eva on the two long-haul flights to New Zealand, and I felt for all parents who had to travel with small children, finally comprehending the stress that they go through to keep their children quiet and well-behaved in an enclosed environment.

Our New Zealand family were thrilled with our arrival, showering Eva with affection and gifts, and it was wonderful to pass her to one of my sisters-in-law or my mother-in-law, knowing that she was in good hands while I had a much-needed break. Everything suddenly seemed to be about babies! I needed to take a step back and try not to feel resentful towards this tiny child who had stolen my independent life, and to change my focus properly onto her. The family time was exactly what I needed. I felt like I was coming out from under a dark veil, and it helped to talk to other women to whom I could relate, sharing stories that made me realise that we were all the same, trying to be 'ideal parents' but not always feeling like we measured up.

Our time in New Zealand was also taken up with dozens of international phone calls, stemming from our initial call to confirm the rental car in New Caledonia. The company had informed us that the online booking price had been a mistake and that they would not honour the contract – the prices was meant to be $150 per day, not per week! We had already purchased our plane tickets to the island, so needed a vehicle; Stuart kept trying to phone to talk to a manager in the office, but they would simply hang up the phone. It took Stuart several days and loads of calls, but he was finally able to track down the head of the regional office and speak with someone who would honour our contract. The only hitch was that we would have to return to the rental car office every week to have the car inspected since we had weekly reservations, rather than having the car for a solid month. Fine.

We drove our newly purchased campervan north, taking the two-hour ferry crossing to Wellington and then driving to Auckland. We flew to New Caledonia and picked up our hired car at the airport, not surprised by the lack of customer service and the rudeness of the staff, and then quickly departed for our adventures. We drove to the east coast and found a great campground site on the beach, surrounded by coconut and mango trees, where we pitched our tent and fell into an easy routine. In the mornings we'd walk the area, collecting at least a dozen fresh mangos that had fallen during the night, enjoying the juicy fruit for breakfast, along with one or two of the fallen coconuts.

Eva was in heaven, devouring the mangos with gusto while covering every square inch of herself in its juices, and we smiled at her delight. We'd swim or snorkel during the day, taking turns building sandcastles with our daughter, and then place Eva in a jolly baby bouncer that we'd attached to a coconut tree that was leaning over the sands of the beach, watching as she'd use her chubby little legs to jump up and down. This was a magical time for us, living simply and with nature, and we felt blessed every day to have this family time and to feel a new level of connection with our active daughter. Eva was now six months old and had changed so dramatically, and we were spellbound as we watched our chubby little Buddha laugh in response to our actions.

It was a simple life, living in a four-man tent with no modern conveniences, but we loved our day-to-day routines. We had fresh water from a tap and fruit from the trees, and Stuart enjoyed scavenging the shores for wood for his nightly campfires, taking pride in building the perfect pyre for us to cook our evening meals or to heat the water for Eva's bath. We had purchased a red bucket and, after making sure that the temperature of the water was just right, we'd place our little girl into the bucket. She was the perfect size to be able to sit inside and play with the water while we washed her down.

Eva now had me under her spell and I finally understood what people were talking about when they spoke of the deep connection between mother and child. I was head over heels in love with my daughter and now simply couldn't imagine life without her. Her laughter, expressive face and chubby little body were so precious to me, and I gained an incredible feeling of happiness just from being in her presence.

We had a wonderful time here, but the highlight had to be our unique wildlife encounter. There was one other family group on the beach with us that day, and when Stuart heard one of the boys say that they had just seen a fin, he ran and got his mask and snorkel and jumped into the water. At first, he wasn't sure whether he was going to see a shark or other large fish – the waters were murky since the mud bottom had been stirred up, but he was shocked when he came right up close to a large, female dugong. I was standing knee-deep on a coral shelf, holding Eva in my arms while trying to find out what Stuart was looking at, and was excited when I saw him surface 20 metres away, screaming 'Dugong!' I had never seen one in the wild before and, as the minutes passed by, I impatiently waited for my husband to change places with me, watching as he'd surface and then disappear, interacting with this threatened species that was the size of a large cow.

Stuart came to me 15 minutes later, swapping his mask and snorkel for Eva, telling me what to look for as I entered the waters. Within less than a minute I came face to face with this three-metre herbivore, enchanted by its proximity and its mannerisms, and we spent several minutes mimicking each other's behaviours. This close encounter was like nothing I'd ever experienced before – two completely different species interacting on a level that both could understand – and it felt like we were dancing together in the warm waters. Stuart and I traded off a couple of more times, spending individual time with this incredible animal, and were honoured by its presence and its interplay. After an hour it left our bay and we returned to sit by our fire, stunned by what we had experienced.

We did venture out from time to time, going on large food shops after our weekly car return, and were able to explore the north, west and south of the island. But each time, since we knew of the paradise location on the east coast, we'd happily return to the same campground. Time flew by and we were sad when our four weeks were up, flying back to New Zealand and finding out some major news by text. We had just bought a house in Lincoln!

We had given Stuart's sister, Louise, power of attorney over our holdings. Prior to us leaving for New Caledonia we had told her that, if needed, we'd help their brother Craig with finances. Craig wasn't able to get a mortgage himself as the banks considered his contracting work unstable. But we were more than shocked when we returned to find out that Craig had found a house and the purchase had been completed. The profit we had made in the last house was now gone, and we were back to living on a restricted budget.

We had returned to the North Island in time for Christmas, finding a campsite on the east coast of the island and enjoying the Christmas morning scenes, watching Santa deliver candy to the boys and girls from the local mail truck. It was our first Christmas as a family of three and we enjoyed the day on the nearby beach, thankful for our health and happiness. We had vowed that a child wouldn't change our style of living, determined to continue to create a life that was drastically different from the norm, and we could hardly believe that we had pulled it off.

We enjoyed a few weeks visiting friends in New Zealand, then drove to Christchurch to join Stuart's mum. We had promised Jan a getaway so, after a quick turnaround, we drove back up the coast to Kaikoura, a small town on the eastern coast of the South Island famous for its marine wildlife, especially its whales and dolphins. Jan had received a gift voucher for a sperm-whale boat trip, so we went to the office and booked a trip for the following day, the only catch being that Eva and I would have to remain on dry land because the vessel wouldn't take children under the age of four.

To say I was envious of the experience that son and mother had that day on the vessel would be a mild understatement. They encountered killer whales, hundreds of dusky dolphins, and – the highlight – four mighty sperm whales. This whale had a number of distinctive characteristics: 1) its large size, being the third largest whale in the world; 2) its teeth, the largest of the toothed variety of whales; and 3) its diving records, being the deepest diving whale on record. And because of the topography of the continental shelf below the seas, this whale was present year-round, searching for its main prey, the squid, and staying within a few kilometres of the coast of the South Island. Stuart and Jan returned from their outing glowing, both trying to downplay the experience so I wouldn't feel so bad, but I was very happy for them.

We left New Zealand bound for the west coast of Australia, where we proudly introduced our daughter to the extended family. We spent one month there, travelling from Uncle Rob's farm to the beaches of the south, borrowing Rob's campervan to camp beside the squeaky white sands, enjoying our time together as we swam in the warm waters and walked the coast. We visited all of Stuart's mother's family, getting together for family barbecues and enjoying the close connection we had with them all.

We left Australia bound for Vancouver, where Stuart and I would depart in separate directions. My husband was bound for the Southern Caribbean, meeting up with Tony and Duncan on the island of Tobago for their three-week boys' trip. Eva and I were travelling to Mexico, going on a package holiday with my mum and dad and my younger sister, Ali. We had a great time in our resort, and it was easy to reconnect with these special people, sharing magical moments with one another.

We returned to Vancouver in time for the 2010 Winter Olympics and were so proud as we watched the Canadian Team. It was to be the first time that Canada would win a gold medal at an Olympic Games that it hosted, as it had failed to do so the two previous times, and our team would finish first overall in gold-medal wins. The city was on a high, and we had so much fun joining my older sister and her family, going to many of the free music events around the town and celebrating Canada's victories with thousands of other revellers. The city was on the world map, being complimented around the world for its tremendous success in hosting the games, and I felt proud to be a Canadian.

Stuart returned from Tobago with a massive smile on his face, having had a great time with the boys, and showed me photos of their time at the week-long carnival there. The participants had worn colourful costumes and the boys had been covered by a variety of paints as they walked the streets, accompanied by calypso drums. We also now learned the great news that Adel was pregnant – all the men from the boys' trip would now be fathers.

We joined Amber up at Whistler Mountain, seeing the infrastructure that had been created for the Winter Olympics, enjoying our time together as we took the gondola to the peak, and going on a number of lake walks.

Our six-month holiday was at an end and we returned to the UK feeling refreshed, looking forward to having our own fridge and beds, and not living out of a suitcase. And within the first few weeks of our return, we received great news: Stuart's boss, Richard, was replacing our old mobile home with a new, modern one, with central heating and double-glazed windows. Our new accommodation was miles better than the last and we felt we were moving up in the world, leaving our backpacker status for a more civilised position.

Chapter 16
The Earth Moved

Returning to work was a challenge. It wasn't that the work was any harder, it was the fact that my daughter hated daycare. Eva would burst into tears as I made my way to the exit after dropping her off, and grabbed onto my legs for dear life. I'd need the help of one of the childcare workers to peel her off me so that I could leave the building. I hated this. The daycare staff would reassure me, saying that a lot of children went through this stage and that Eva would stop crying after the first five minutes, but I sometimes just couldn't believe that was the case. My heart would be in my throat as I walked from the building, trying my best not to burst into tears myself as I felt my daughter's pain of separation, and I'd pray that she'd get over this stage quickly.

Once I was at school, Eva had to be pushed to the back of my mind as I focused on what I was teaching that day, making sure that my lessons were ready and that I had all necessary equipment for the science experiments. I had been asked back for a fourth consecutive year to a wonderful country school on the coast, where I knew the students and staff, and where my good friend Naomi was my co-worker. We'd spend our lunch breaks together, making plans for the weekends and our summer days, and making time for barbecues, beach time and music festivals.

The time flew by; suddenly the summer holidays were upon us, and Eva and I were heading across the Atlantic, bound for Canada.

The Canadian summer was brilliant for us. The sun was out in full force, and I moved a number of times between my parents' place on Bowen and the summer cabin on Pasley Island. Eva was now one year old and she loved following my two nieces, Emma and Sofia, wherever they went, so this influenced my whereabouts – it was always easier when there were more people about. All the children on the island seemed to congregate together, forming a posse as they moved from one location to another. It was brilliant to watch the interaction of the group, with the older kids taking the smallest children under their wings.

In the last week of my visit, my parents kindly took Eva off my hands so that I could be a bridesmaid at my soul sister's wedding, up on the Sunshine Coast. Amber, my girlfriend who I had worked with up at the fishing lodge and then travelled and worked with in New Zealand, had met her match in Dave, and was now going to tie the knot and settle down. She had organised an incredible three-day event at a spectacular seaside venue, and it was great to be a part of all the action. It was the first time that I had been on my own since having Eva and, although I would never go back in time to change anything, it felt wonderful to feel like me again, a strong individual able to direct my life as I chose. And I recognised that I now had the best of both worlds, happily returning to my beautiful daughter and loving family at the end of the celebrations, and then leaving a few days later to join my wonderful husband.

Whenever I returned from my Canadian summer holiday we started to make a plan for our six months away. We would need to be in New Zealand for Christmas this time, where Marie and Kirsten wanted to join us for three weeks during their winter holidays. This would be an epic trip for them, being the first time Marie would meet her grandmother, aunts, uncles and the large number of first cousins. With this in mind, we organised travelling first to Malaysia, then New Zealand and Australia, and finishing off in Canada.

Our first stop would be the island of Langkawi in the Andaman Sea, located off the mainland coast of northwestern Malaysia. After our first night in very basic accommodation, Stuart scoured the beaches until he found the best place for our family of three, bargaining hard to keep the cost down, with the trump card that we would be staying for four weeks. I was over the moon when he brought us to the hotel located in the Oriental Village, a themed open-air complex with a huge lake in the centre, surrounded by an art gallery, animal exhibits, shops and loads of restaurants. It would take mere minutes to travel from our room to a number of different activities, from feeding and riding on elephants and having close encounters with deer, rabbits and ducks, to coming within feet of and even touching a tiger.

We visited the Malaysian Tiger exhibit daily, since it was steps from our hotel. The tiger there could be viewed via a wall of glass, with a reflective mirror on the tiger's side, and we'd observe as he watched himself, so close that we could see the colour of his eyes. The lady staff member was always very friendly and informative and, after a few weeks of our daily visits, asked if we'd like to go into the restricted area to feed the tiger ourselves! We jumped at the opportunity and were led to a back room, with a metal netting separating us from this beautiful cat, and were amazed when we were given a bucket of chicken legs to pass through the fence. We were able to touch the tiger's coat as he rubbed along the thin barrier, and it was thrilling to watch his large teeth and jaws as he took the chicken from our hands. An incredible experience.

If we wanted to go a little further afield, we would walk to the nearby waterfall, jumping into the chilly pool at its base. Or we would take the gondola up to the Langkawi Sky Bridge – a 125-metre, curved, cable-stayed pedestrian bridge, 2,300 feet above sea level – from where we could admire the spectacular scenery of the rainforest as it meandered down to the sea. Our hotel was also associated with a four-star hotel on the beach, allowing us to use its facilities, and we often took the five-minute shuttle to this location, enjoying the large pool with its own waterfall, or jumping from the warm golden sands into the crystal waters of the Andaman Sea.

Eva was a little star, strutting around like she owned the place, having photograph after photograph taken of her as she stood out from the locals. At first she shied away from the camera, lowering her head and saying 'No!' But by the end of the month she had changed her ways, putting on her biggest smile and striking funny poses to satisfy the photographer. If we had had a dollar for every time she was photographed, I would be a rich mama.

We had such an incredible time here that we didn't want to leave. But we knew exciting times awaited us in New Zealand, with our eldest daughter joining in on the fun. We also had a new secret to impart – pregnancy tests were telling us I was pregnant – so looked forward to passing on the news at Christmas time, as we had when we had had Eva in the belly. Both Stuart and I come from large families and couldn't imagine the life of a single child, so we hoped to add one more individual to our clan, rounding our number to an even four.

We returned to New Zealand and spent the first few days with Stuart's mother, Jan, reassured that she had recovered from the shock of the September 4th Canterbury earthquake, the epicentre of which had been directly below her feet. Luckily, her new little house had survived the shake and she was in great spirits, loving now having little Eva to entertain and excited about the arrival of her German granddaughter. During this time we contacted a midwife in the area, scheduling in an ultrasound scan to make sure everything was on track with our growing baby. I felt very happy with the slight bump that was starting to show under my t-shirt. We also spent a few days searching for a car, and finally bought a sedan large enough to hold five people and all our luggage.

We picked Marie and Kirsten up from Christchurch International Airport, pleased that they were finally on New Zealand soil but upset when we heard that Marie had been ill for most of the journey, due to motion sickness. We brought her back to Grandma's place and within a few days she was back to her spirited and happy self, working on her English and playing with her younger sister.

We then travelled south to Stuart's sister's place, a beautiful farm with stunning, 360-degree panoramic views. We were grateful as Louise and Ian welcomed us in, creating a space for all of us to rest our heads.

We formed a large clan by the time Christmas Day appeared. Stuart's eldest brother, Garry, arrived with his two children, Deana and Mitch, and then we welcomed Craig and Vicki and their two boys, Matthew and Joshua, with whom I had a close connection, since they had joined us in the UK for a couple of seasons a few years earlier. And then there was our family, our hosts, Louise and Ian, and their two kids, Stacey and Ryan. Completing our circle was Jan, who joined us for a few nights. She was immediately kidnapped by the younger generation, going out for walks and treasure hunts, appearing like the Pied Piper and enjoying her time with her grandkids.

The festivities began as we all congregated together and I was relieved when we had at last announced my pregnancy – my sisters-in-law and I always enjoyed our wine together, and they had been suspicious when I held back from the refills. The adults would stay up until the early hours of the morning, playing pool, darts and air hockey, or just drinking at the bar in the 'Man Cave', the double-car garage, which had been outfitted for entertainment. I became the night-time babysitter for Eva while Stuart enjoyed the rare moments of being together with all his siblings, and I felt like an old maid, coming out at 4 am in my pyjamas to berate them – the dartboard was situated on the other side of the wall where I laid my head, and all I could hear as I tried to sleep was the 'thunk' as the darts hit the board.

I phoned my family to wish them all a merry Christmas and told them of our baby news. Everyone was extremely excited, and then it was my turn to be surprised. Ali told me she was going to get married to Dan, a man she'd moved in with a few months earlier, and that they were planning on tying the knot that August up at Pasley Island. Uh oh. Problem. This was the same month that our baby was due, which meant that I wouldn't be able to be at her wedding, since women aren't allowed to fly in the last month of pregnancy. Damn. Ali and I both hung up the phone, elated at each other's news but saddened by the thought that I wouldn't be in attendance for her nuptials.

During the following days we went on day trips, visiting the south shores of Oamaru to see the blue penguin colony, and walking on the beaches to inspect the famous Moeraki boulders. After New Year, our family of five went on a one-week tour of the South Island. We travelled from the southerly Milford Sound Fjordland to the west coast, then hiked to the base of Franz Josef Glacier, enveloped in scenery that always takes my breath away. Marie's English had improved by leaps and bounds, and we all had a great time exploring her father's native country together.

It felt like no time before the three weeks were up and we were taking Marie and Kirsten to the airport for their flights back to Germany. Next we stayed with Craig and Vicki in their/our newly renovated home. Then in our last remaining days we moved to Stuart's mum's place, where she enjoyed precious moments with Eva, as well as imploring us to promise to return the following year with the new baby. Stuart and I went into the city for our ultrasound scan, surprised when we found out that we were not as far along as we thought – our due date had changed by six weeks, indicating that we had probably miscarried the first child and immediately got pregnant again.

It was at this time that I spoke to Ali, finding out that she and Dan had completely changed their plans for me, bringing their wedding date forward from August to March, and that they were now going to get married in Mexico. My mum and dad were on the case, organising rooms and flights for everyone, and we jumped at the chance to go to a five-star, all-inclusive resort with 30 of our closest friends and relatives. Luckily, we had already planned to end our six-month trip in Canada, so this one-week trip to Mexico worked in perfectly.

We packed up our multiple bags, stroller and car seat, and headed for our next destination, the west coast of Australia. There we were collected by Rick and Lisa and their four children, in their six-berth motor home. Rick and Lisa had been Stuart's first host parents when he left New Zealand at 18 years of age, and he had worked on their farm in Alberta, Canada, for two summer seasons before moving to the UK. They had remained good friends ever since, attending our wedding and our week-long after-party up at Pasley, as well as visiting us in Devon over the years. And now here we were all together – four adults and five children – sitting in their large motor home, laughing as we chaotically tried to exit Perth's international airport, clattering over speed bumps and at one point heading in the wrong direction.

Rick drove us south to Uncle Rob's farm, where we were able to relax and enjoy each other's company. We filled our time with walks on the farm, going to the gorgeous beaches and to some of the numerous wineries, where we danced to the live music while sampling a variety of bottles. We'd have barbecues in the evening, watching as the kangaroos congregated on the fields below us, and listening to Rob as he entertained us with his amazing poetry, verses that he had created and kept in his memory. Rick and his family left after a week, bound for the east coast, along the southern highway. We soon followed in their footsteps, borrowing Uncle Rob's van, which was fitted out with bed, sink and cooker, and heading to the spectacular scenery in the south of the country.

Australia's south west coastline changed along our route, from tranquil bays fringed by sandy white beaches, to rugged granite headlands and cliffs. We were delighted to witness the beauty of this region and spent many happy hours on the shoreline, building sandcastles with Eva or hiking over the rocks to find secluded bays where we'd skinny-dip and lie naked in the sands. By late afternoon we'd be searching our maps to find a campground, pleased when we'd set up camp and found the shower block, happy to have a warm shower to wash off the salt of the sea.

It was during this trip that it happened. We were just walking up from a day on the beach when I felt wetness between my legs, and not knowing whether I'd just peed myself (which isn't uncommon during pregnancy), I immediately found a secluded spot to investigate further. I was completely devastated when I saw all the blood. I'd heard of other women bleeding during pregnancy, so didn't want to assume the worst-case scenario, but I couldn't help feeling disheartened.

Stuart and I drove the following day to the nearest hospital, and after many hours of waiting for the arrival of the one and only man who performed ultrasound scans, we had our results. Our little baby had no heartbeat so was no longer viable, and I could expect for the foetus to dislodge and come out on its own at any time. It had been so easy to conceive and carry Eva that I had assumed that things would be the same with our next child, and I was devastated to hear that I was no longer going to have this baby. It took me some time to get over this loss. I also felt awful knowing that I had caused my younger sister to change her wedding venue and date after she had learned that I was going to have a baby. It took all my willpower to force myself to count my blessings rather than focus on the negative experience, repeating over and over to myself that everything happens for the right reason and that this was meant to be. I knew that we were blessed to have Eva, aware that so many people have the misfortune of not being able to conceive or carry even one child to full-term, and I used Eva now as my source of comfort, cocooning myself in her love and innocence.

We drove back to Rob's farm, returning to his loving embrace and kind words, and my energy returned as time passed, healing my heart and rekindling my spirit. One of the worst parts of this whole experience was having to make all the international phone calls, letting our family know what had transpired and hearing their sympathy and commiseration. Ali was brilliant, offering her support over the phone, telling me I was crazy to feel guilty about her wedding and reassuring me about how excited they all were about next month's nuptials in Mexico.

By the end of the month I felt better in spirit, but not in my body. My girth was still expanding, with my body believing that it was still pregnant since the foetus had not yet been expelled. This wreaked havoc with my emotions – I couldn't let go of losing my baby because my body literally wouldn't let go.

We had moved on to Perth and were staying with Stuart's cousin when we saw the headline news on TV that Christchurch had suffered another earthquake, this one much more destructive as it was centred very close to the surface and had happened during working hours. We watched with tears in our eyes as individuals were interviewed, breaking down over the deaths of their loved ones or expressing their desperation over friends and relatives still trapped in the damaged buildings, some of them having to be held back to prevent them going in to the unsafe conditions to try themselves to rescue people. The body count started to climb and we were amazed by the aerial footage of the city that showed the devastation of this 6.3 magnitude earthquake. We contacted all our New Zealand family members and were so thankful that they were all accounted for, but we could feel their pain for the loss of their home town and the damage to their individual homes.

We flew from Perth to Vancouver, immediately seeking more news on the earthquake, and could barely believe that the earth's movement could change the landscape so severely. Christchurch was no longer a viable city; its iconic cathedral, along with multiple other buildings, had been severely impaired, and the damage had been exacerbated by the weakened infrastructure caused by the September earthquake and its aftershocks. Significant liquefaction affected the region, producing around 400,000 tonnes of silt that prevented rebuilding or repairs and caused thousands of individuals to lose their homes and livelihoods. Stuart was devastated as he saw on TV the aftermath affecting his home town. My heart went out to him and all his countrymen, with 185 people confirmed dead and so many families suffering.

But as the days progressed, we had another focus to attend to – Ali was getting married to Dan. They first had a civil ceremony at my grandmother's home, inviting 50 of their closest family and friends to join the celebration, after which we sped downtown to continue celebrating. We had great fun with all our cousins and it was wonderful to be surrounded by so much love.

Less than a week later, 30 of us boarded a charter plane that transported us down to Ixtapa, Mexico. It didn't take us long to settle into a routine at our luxurious accommodation, gathering together by the poolside and ordering our first drinks by 10 am. The all-inclusive resort had multiple restaurants, swim-up bars and a number of waiters that constantly brought us drinks. We laughed as we watched some of our party members participate in the water aerobics and water spin-classes, or become opposing team members in the competitive water polo matches.

The day of the wedding was wonderful. My parents, sisters and I all sipped champagne and gathered in the honeymoon suite, watching as Ali had her hair and make-up done and admiring how stunning she looked in her wedding dress. Eva and my nieces, Emma and Sofia, were dressed in gorgeous flower-girl outfits and the three of them looked like little angels as they chased each other around the room. Then we moved to the outdoor venue along the seaside, walking the length of the dock to reach the arched podium, which was strewn with beautiful flowers.

After the 'I dos', Dan and Ali went onto the beach and proceeded to walk into the waves, their photographer directing them in her shots, while we all watched from our high perch, smiling at their antics and so happy for their union. After a quick change from their wet clothes, we all met for a delicious dinner and then danced long into the night, with our own private DJ. It was a magical time, being surrounded by our closest friends and family, and we all made the most of our time together in this exotic clime, feeling blessed to be a part of this tribe.

On one of the following days, my two younger sisters hired a fishing boat for the day and invited a group of us on to the water. We spent hours trolling for a catch; while we didn't get a single bite, we saw beautiful scenery and enjoyed some great wildlife viewing, including bird colonies and dolphins riding at our bow. But the highlight was when we came within metres of a massive, dark object at the surface of the water. The captain shook his head, saying he thought it looked like the man-eating tiger shark, and everyone thought Stuart was crazy as he stripped off his shirt and got ready to jump in. He had recognised the large fish, and jumped in beside the whale shark, a large filter feeder, which none of my companions had seen before. I smiled as they compared him to Steve Irwin, saying how impressed they were with his animal knowledge. Stuart stayed swimming with this gentle giant for a few minutes before it submerged into the depths.

While we were in Mexico we also celebrated my older sister's 40th birthday, surprising her when she came to the dinner table to find all 30 of us all wearing the same shirt, with her face on the front. She was completely shocked to see us all and we all smiled at the huge grin that remained on her face for the duration of the night.

Before we left, my family accompanied Weeze and her family as they had a 'dolphin encounter'. Emma was placed in one group and Sofia and Weeze in another, and we watched as they entered large pools, immediately surrounded by dozens of bottlenose dolphins, which were then directed by their trainers to perform a number of activities. It was incredible to watch these intelligent mammals as they executed their routine for over half an hour, but I also felt bad that they were in captivity for the sole purpose of human entertainment.

Our time was up and we all headed to the international airport. It had been a very successful week away, and I counted my blessings as we returned to Vancouver, knowing that I had so much to be thankful for. I had an amazing family, both in Canada and New Zealand, and everyone was safe, healthy and stable. The only problem I had was internal – my body, with the foetus still in place, still believed I was pregnant. I was growing by the day, having to switch into my maternity gear to get comfortable for the long-haul flight back to the UK.

Chapter 17
New Roots

It was a month before I would finally have the operation to remove the dead foetus, and I tried to detach myself from the whole procedure, knowing that I'd only hurt myself by focusing on the death of our child. I knew I should feel pleased that it had happened at this early stage rather than further down the track. I knew I was lucky to have Eva in my life, and I would always be thankful that I had my healthy, beautiful daughter, as well as my step-daughter Marie.

I filled my UK time with activities, travelling down to Devon during the half-term break to meet up with Adel and Tony and spending time with Marci, who was pregnant, Blue and Sonny. I loved our cliff walks and the rugged shoreline of this county, a complete contradiction to the incredibly flat vista of Norfolk to which I returned. I also made more plans with my girlfriends Naomi and Wendy, filling up my weekends and exploring more of the countryside, discovering new locations that fuelled my spirit.

Eva and I travelled to Canada for our summer holiday, and after three weeks with my sisters, cousins, mother and two best friends, Sarah and Amber (who was eight months pregnant), I returned in great spirits. My great friend Marci had given birth to a little girl, Florence, while I was away, and I was excited for their family of four, a 'complete unit'. I looked forward to the end of our season – Stuart had given me full rein on this year's travel plans, and I had a great time deciding the countries I wanted to visit and in which order.

But before our six-month family holiday, Eva and I would become tourists in our own country. My mum and dad came over for a September visit and I acted as their guide as we drove north and west, visiting York, the Lake District and the Peak District in our round trip. We had a great time – I find it extremely easy to travel with my parents, and we all were entranced by the history and changing scenery as we covered hundreds of miles. We returned to Norfolk, having a few more days together at home base, and made plans to see each other again in Panama, Central America, which was to be one of our stops in our upcoming travels.

Before we left, I received a call from Amber to say that she had had a little boy, whom they had named Brodie, and asking if I would be his godmother. Amber was one of Eva's godmothers and I loved the idea of tying our families together forever. After a tearful conversation and acceptance of my new role, I hung up the phone, elated by the arrival of her healthy baby boy and by the role I would play in his life.

Stuart and I continued to try to conceive again and were overjoyed when a pregnancy test confirmed our suspicions. We kept the secret close to our hearts as we didn't want to get our hopes up, only to be disappointed if I were to miscarry again.

Before our six months of travel we flew to Germany to visit Kirsten and Marie in their new home, a beautiful, spacious apartment overlooking a massive forest. There we enjoyed daily walks in the woods, following the dirt trails as they crisscrossed under the massive canopy.

Unfortunately, the day before we left for our six months away, I started to bleed again. I tried desperately not to show my heartache as I felt my dream of another child being swept away, focusing instead on the travel ahead – we had many miles to cross and many hours of travel before our first destination. Our first port of call was Boracay Island in the Philippines, a tropical haven known to be one of the most beautiful islands in the world, surrounded by stunning, powdery white sand against azure water. I had seen pictures of the boys' trip to this location and had wanted ever since to see it for myself, setting an entire month aside for this section of the voyage.

After multiple flights, stopovers and a boat ride, we finally arrived on the small island and took a motorised tricycle to our one night of pre-booked accommodation, a budget backpacker hostel on the east coast. Stuart worked his magic, and by the next day had booked us in to a four-star resort, located at the northern tip of the famous White Beach. Our new accommodation comprised a gorgeous, large suite with a small kitchenette, allowing us to save money by eating some of our meals at home.

The days flowed into one another as we enjoyed our new surroundings, heading to the beach in the morning and spending hours every day in the warm waters. We watched as Eva made friends with the local boys and girls, building sandcastles, playing frisbee and kicking a ball to one another. We'd return to our suite for lunch, taking turns to walk to a local shop and returning with food for delicious family meals. After Eva's nap we'd either return to the beach and walk down its 4 km length, then explore the numerous shops in the commercial centre, or we'd go to the resort's luxury pool, spending hours in the fresh water. We made time for diving, visiting some of the more popular underwater sights. We spent one afternoon out on the water, sitting under sails as we glided across the turquoise sea, holding Eva close as we admired the beauty of the bay from a different perspective.

Our time was also taken up with property hunting – my cousin Margot was part of a team selling a development in North Vancouver, and we had also seen a real-estate listing of a great house on Bowen Island. We were keen to invest our money somewhere since the UK bank was giving us an interest rate of less than one per cent. After much deliberation, paperwork and faxing, at the very last minute we pulled out of a deal on a great apartment, knowing that we were on the knife-edge of financially being able to pull it off.

During our last days on the island, our attention was focused on the television set – the Rugby World Cup was on and the New Zealand All Blacks were battling their way to top position. Stuart had avidly followed the six-week event, which was being held in New Zealand, studying which of the 20 countries made it through to the next stage and which were eliminated, and things started to get tense as we got closer to the quarter-finals and to the final game. We had gone to one of the bars for a quarter- final game, Stuart and Eva dressed in their patriotic All Blacks tops, supporting Stuart's homeland, and were ecstatic when they won that round. But Stuart now wanted to focus on the deciding game without any distractions, so we watched it on the TV at home. Stuart was glued to every play as the New Zealand All Blacks took on their arch-rivals from France, the team that had knocked them out of the competition in an epic game four years earlier. Needless to say, you could cut the tension with a knife as he followed the game, and time seemed to slow down as the battle was fought. I was so pleased and Stuart was ecstatic when the final buzzer signalled the end of the game, with New Zealand winning the tournament, defeating France with a score of 8–7.

It wasn't long before we set off again, heading for the Indonesian island of Bali. Although I had been there before, I had never explored the north or east coast, so I had booked us into a lovely resort for a two-week period on the north coast. We were happy with our accommodation, spending our days by the pool, but had to stay off the black sands of the beach during the peak of the day – the sands were so hot that they would scorch our bare feet, resulting in painful blisters.

After a relaxing two weeks we travelled to the east coast, finding a great seaside resort with an amazing reef on its doorstep. We took turns at snorkelling, having close encounters with reef sharks and coral fish, and carrying sticks with us as protection from attacks from the territorial trigger fish. Stuart had been the first of us to encounter the local trigger fish, receiving a painful bite to his big toe when he swam too close to their nest, and he made sure we were well armed before re-entering the water.

We rented a motorbike and drove to a spot 10 kilometres from our accommodation, stopping to snorkel at a shipwreck that was only 30 metres from shore. We loved the feeling of being back in warm waters and surrounded by loads of species of fish. I was in heaven in Bali, thanks not only to the scenery in and out of the water, but due to the Indonesian fruit. We would pay one of the waiters to bring us bags of fruit, and the three of us would dive into the lychees, mangos and, my personal favourite, mangosteens.

With just one week left on Bali, we headed back to the main city of Kuta, stopping off at Bali Safari & Marine Park for a one-night stay, as a treat for our wedding anniversary. We arrived at the Mara River Safari Lodge in the park and were immediately transferred to our thatched dwelling where, as we opened the screen doors to the outside fenced deck, we were amazed and delighted to find zebras, wildebeest, oryxes and white rhinos inhabiting the landscape only a few metres away.

After throwing all the fresh vegetables, which were supplied in the room, to the African mammals, we set off to explore the grounds of the park, mapping out the areas that we wanted to be sure not to miss and noting the times of the different events taking place on-site. Our package included passes to go on a 'Safari Journey', and we tracked down the location of the start of the tour, excited to continue our African wildlife encounters. We boarded the large truck and began our 30-minute tour, taking numerous photos of the animals living in the replicated habitats of Indonesia, India and Africa. Eva was on cloud nine as we passed lions and tigers, hippos and crocodiles, dramatically pointing out the huge number of different animals as we passed, trying to take photos of every single creature in the park.

We returned to our accommodation after a final look around the park, then went for a brief dip in the resort swimming pool to cool off from the heat and humidity of the day. We couldn't believe our eyes as we stood chest-deep in the refreshing water and watched the elephants, rhinos and wildebeest grazing on the grass only a few metres away. Unbelievable.

One of the advantages of staying at this resort was that we could go into the park at any time, since the lodge was situated inside the gated, fenced perimeter. We were over the moon when we turned one corner to find three orangutans ambling across the pavement, following their trainer. We reached for our cameras and Stuart moved forward, positioning himself in close proximity to the amazing animals. It wasn't long before one approached him and held his hand, taking Stuart's baseball cap from his head and putting it on himself. A few hours later we had another close encounter, having one orangutan positioned on my lap for a professional photo, with Eva, a little uncertain about this hairy stranger, sitting beside us.

We followed the schedule, making sure we were present for the multiple animal-feeding times around the park, and then setting aside time to have a close encounter with a young lion, amazed as we were allowed to stroke the fur on its back. We fed elephants by hand and watched a great performance with the majestic animals, a show that described the conflict between man and elephants over natural resources, and what we humans need to do to make it work for all concerned. We had an amazing time at the Bali Safari & Marine Park and looked forward to our next adventures in Africa, knowing that Eva would love spotting the animals in their natural, wild setting.

Before leaving the island, we spent a day at Bali's Waterbom water park. We had received a gift voucher when we attended a 'timeshare session', during which salesmen had pressurised us to part with $20,000 to invest in a 'golden opportunity', and where the intensity of their sales pitch had made us come very close to handing over the money. Luckily, we had removed ourselves before getting tied into a scheme that wouldn't work for our lifestyle, and had been happy when we had left only with free passes for the water park. We spent a great day together at the park, and Eva and Stuart had a grand time going on ride after ride, happy in each other's company while I took photos of them. I watched as Stuart walked up flights of stairs on his own, waiting patiently in line to go on a death-defying slide, one which my brother-in-law, Dan, had helped design. Eva and I laughed, watching Stuart's expression as he fell down the engineered slide with massive velocity. I had to hold back on the extreme rides – the pregnancy test was confirming yet again that I was pregnant – but enjoyed watching my husband and daughter as they raced from one ride to the other.

We left Indonesia bound for Taiwan. This hadn't originally been one of the places I wanted to see but, since it was a stopover on our flight, we extended our time there to a week to explore the island. Unfortunately, as Taiwan is in a northerly latitude, the December days were cold and wet. This was in complete contrast to the climes of the two previous months and we were ill-equipped for the weather, immediately purchasing rain jackets, sweaters, trousers and shoes for all of us. We discovered delectable bakeries a few blocks from our four-star hotel and would make daily trips there, purchasing a wide variety of freshly baked delights and bringing bags of food home with us. Before leaving Taiwan we took the train to the capital, Taipei, where we were amazed by all the neon billboards covering the facades of the buildings, and by the density of people on the city streets.

But then it was time to move again, heading to Vancouver for Christmas with the family, where we once again announced that I was pregnant. We joined Weeze and her family up at Whistler Mountain for New Year, and Eva had a blast as she followed my nieces, Emma and Sofia, loving every moment as they took her under their wing and made a big fuss over her. Our best day in Whistler was when we all went to the Tube Park. Here you can have hours of fun, speeding on giant, tyre-like rings down snow slides set into Blackcomb Mountain. I watched as everyone cruised down the 1,000-foot lanes, the wind in their faces, with Eva sitting on her own child-size tube and Stuart hanging on to her tube as they whipped down the side of the mountain.

We returned to the city and stayed with my sister Ali, who was now pregnant, setting aside time to spend with my other sister, Sasha, and organising dinners with our cousins. During this time, Stu and I left Eva in my sister's care in order to have an ultrasound scan. We entered the medical building apprehensively, with me drinking the required litres of water to fill my bladder. I was led off on my own for the examination and scan, lying on the hospital bed as they placed the jelly-covered instrument onto my stomach, keeping the monitor from my view as they analysed what they were seeing.

As the minutes passed and the nurse's face looked perplexed, I tried not to get disheartened. I had been in this position before and aimed to remain as positive as possible now. I asked if the child was viable and the response was affirmative, but she kept asking me about my dates and whether I'd had any previous miscarriages. Finally, she revealed the first of three major discoveries: my child was not in the 11th–12th week as I had thought – its size was indicating that it had developed to 18 weeks. What?! This didn't make sense, and I immediately asked for Stuart to join me. He came into the room, concern written all over his face; I reassured him that everything was alright, just that we had our dates wrong. We discussed this possibility, knowing that the date would bring us back to a September conception, and openly talked in front of the nurse about the miscarriage I had had while in Germany. And then the nurse revealed the second discovery: that my viable child had had a twin and that she could see the empty sack beside it. A twin!!

The nurse was also shocked, saying that in the 20 years of performing this procedure, she'd never seen it where one twin miscarried but the other one held on, continuing to grow as normal in the belly. Wow. So we were lucky that this little one had stayed with us, a sign that he or she clearly wanted to be a part of our family. And then for the third discovery. Since we were now 18 weeks into the pregnancy, the nurse said she could tell us the gender of the child if we wanted to know, asking us if we had made any guesses. As I had three sisters, all but one of my first cousins were girls, and we already had Eva, I told the nurse that I already 'knew' the sex of my child, that it was a girl. She asked if I wanted her to confirm this, and after some deliberation with Stu, we said yes. She placed the hand-piece of the monitor over my belly and proceeded to show us the outline of the baby. And there, between the two small legs was a clear outline of our baby's appendage – a penis and ball sack were easy to distinguish on the black-and-white screen. We were going to have a boy! A boy! What was I going to do with a boy?! Seriously, even with the news of the new due date and the fact that I had been carrying twins, it was the news of a boy that completely threw me. Oh my goodness.

We left the medical centre, so happy that we were still pregnant and that the baby was healthy, and returned to Ali's place, making the calls to let everyone in on our news.

Within a week we were off once more, taking a flight to Los Angeles, California. There we reunited with Paige, who had been my best friend in high school and the one responsible for helping me push my boundaries, following in her footsteps to the Club Med in Mexico and then going to Langara Island Fishing Lodge in the Queen Charlotte Islands to help her brother. It was a perfect reunion and we were able to re-establish our close bonds, happy to be in each other's presence, especially as Paige was now going through a tough time in her life, experiencing a nasty divorce and with two small children in the balance. After a week of together time, we said our goodbyes and boarded our flight bound for Panama, Central America.

I had been to Costa Rica with an ex-boyfriend in 1992, and we had crossed south over the border to Panama, spending time on the islands of Bocas del Toro on the Caribbean coast. But I wasn't prepared for the scene that unfolded this time as we came in to land, stunned by the large number of skyscrapers and buildings under our wings. We had organised a car and driver to pick us up and transport us down the coast to our rented apartment in Playa Coronado, and I was astounded as we drove through Panama City, looking out at all the modern buildings, casinos, hotels and massive mall complexes, and stunned as we passed the newly built Trump Towers. This was not the Central America that I had known.

We arrived at our beachfront accommodation, at the Coronado Country Club, where three large apartment towers formed the backdrop and overlooked the largest swimming pool in Latin America, encircled by large villas within the landscaped grounds. It was the perfect place to chill out, and we were poolside most mornings and afternoons, before venturing out front to the beach and walking ten minutes down the sands to buy fresh fish and large prawns at the local fish market.

There were loads of expats here, mainly Canadian and American retirees coming down to escape the harsh winters back home, and they all seemed to congregate in this part of Panama. One morning, as we entertained Eva at the pool, we met a Canadian woman whose first question to me was 'Do you rent or own your apartment?' The idea of investing in property here hadn't even entered my mind, but after hearing of the growth of Panama, especially since the Americans had handed over ownership of the very profitable Panama Canal in 1999, my interest was piqued. We started to look around the area, visiting real-estate offices and picking up flyers on specific properties, and then driving up and down the coast to look at the units.

We viewed some of the high-rise apartments in the neighbouring buildings and loved the large suites and the views that we saw, but neither Stuart nor I enjoyed the vertiginous feeling from being so high up, and we continued our search nearer ground level. And then my mum and dad arrived. It didn't take them long to change from their warm clothing into swimsuits then join us down at the pool and beach, loving the time to play with their granddaughter. We became tourists together, travelling up to Panama City and taking a city tour on a double-decker open-top bus, watching as we passed incredible sights and learned about the history of the region.

Panama was in a boom period – while most other countries had suffered in the recession of 2007, this country had come out on top, enjoying an annual 10–12 per cent growth, and we were amazed at how the government was creating such a strong infrastructure within the country. We learned that, due to its uniquely positioned geography, Panama was becoming an economic giant on the world stage – the canal slashed shipping costs and provided the country with a large, steady, dependable income, contributing more than 10 per cent of the GDP. Panama was also one of the Western Hemisphere's major economic centres, and was an attractive alternative to the floundering US for anyone looking for financial stability and flexibility. By the end of the tour we were all very impressed by this Latin American country, as they were pumping in money to support their healthcare sector, education system and ICT development, as well as being listed by highly ranked magazines like *The New Yorker* and *Forbes* as the number-one place to retire.

We returned to Coronado and continued with our property search, but within a few days felt that our time was being taken over by viewings, preventing us from enjoying our holiday as a family. So Stuart and I put a stop to our search, asking the real-estate office only to let us know if anything special came up. We were told that there was one incredible deal out on the market, but that a gentleman from the Canadian Embassy was due to come in that afternoon to sign the contract, having spent the last two weeks with his lawyers ensuring that everything was legitimate. If he didn't show up by the end of the day, they would let us know.

The next day we received the call to say that the other man hadn't shown up, so my mum, dad, Stuart, Eva and I followed our realtor Jodi's car to a Golf and Beach Resort. We drove through the manned security gates, past the 18-hole golf course and towards two small towers located 100 metres from the beach. We all squeezed into the small elevator and waited in anticipation as Jodi opened the door to the third-floor unit, where we scouted out the fully furnished apartment.

My heart was racing as I finished my perusal – this apartment struck a chord in me. The large, three-bedroom, four-bathroom suite was furnished beautifully, with teak furniture, flatscreen TVs, and a massive fridge/freezer unit with its own ice maker. It had high ceilings and a maid's quarters, but the best part was the view from the front deck: uninterrupted vistas of the Pacific Ocean, dotted with small fishing boats from the neighbouring fishing village. I loved it! Stuart approached me, raising his eyebrows in question, and I nodded my head. This was it.

After we had taken in the fact that this was a turn-key apartment, meaning that everything, from furniture to linens, high-end dishware to professional knives, was included, we exited the building and walked down the road to the beach club. We passed the golf shop and restaurant, passing manicured lawns as we walked down towards the massive infinity pool, with the backdrop of the beautiful white sandy beach and the rippling Pacific. Wow, simply the best spot we had seen.

We returned home, the four adults discussing the pros and cons of the deal and, with more questions surfacing in our heads in terms of the logistics of buying property in a foreign country, we phoned the realtor and requested that we meet up with her in a few hours. She tried to put us off, with it being Saturday afternoon, but eventually agreed to see us, and it wasn't long before we were in her office, getting our answers and putting our bid on to the table. We wanted it. And within 24 hours we heard back from the vendor. We had made ourselves a deal.

On Monday morning we were informed that the man from the Canadian Embassy had returned to the realtors' office with the intention of going ahead with the purchase of the property. But unfortunately for him, our deal was already in motion ... and we now had just three weeks to find the money. My mum and dad left after their two weeks were up, excited about our new investment and already discussing the best time to return to the sunny climes. It was touch and go there for a while – we came close to losing the deal entirely, literally coming to the final hour before the money arrived into the lawyer's bank account.

Boy did we celebrate once we knew we had it! We also had another cause for celebration – my sister Ali had had a baby boy, little Benjamin, and mummy and baby were healthy and happy. Luck was shining down on all our lives.

We left Panama after two months in the country, extremely happy with our new home, and we looked forward to returning in the fall, when we would have two small children in tow. At six months pregnant, my stomach was growing ever larger and I felt great, but our holiday wasn't over yet – we still had the Big Apple to explore. I had never been to New York City before and I was looking forward to going to Times Square and Central Park, places that I'd seen hundreds of times on TV.

I had reserved a hotel away from the city centre, one that had an airport-shuttle service, and was pleased that we had an easy transition from the airport to our accommodation. It was heaven when I sank into the warm bath, away from the chilly temperature outside. My first cousin, Sarah, and her husband, Brian, had travelled down from their home in Cambridge, where they both worked at Harvard University. They joined us with their children, Maddie and Brayden, meeting us the following morning at the hotel restaurant.

We all took the train into the downtown area, then jumped on to a 'hop-on/hop-off double-decker tour', which transported us to all the famous sites in the area. From the Statue of Liberty to the Empire State Building and the Rockefeller Center, we toured around the city streets, listening to the guide as he listed facts and figures, providing fascinating, detailed information about the region. We went for walks in Central Park and visited the American Museum of Natural History, fascinated by the extensive exhibits, but not coming close to viewing their collection of over 30 million specimens and artefacts.

Sarah and her clan left us on Sunday evening, and we had the opportunity to meet up with a fellow backpacker, a beautiful Israeli girl called Shani. She had rented a room from us for a week on Roatán Island, Honduras, and Stuart had helped her to gain confidence in the water, teaching her the specifics of scuba diving. Shani became our host and benefactor in New York, taking us out to dinner at a famous pasta house that was just a few steps from Times Square. We were all amazed when Eva curled up on the large sofa seat there and fell asleep – we had to shout at one another to be heard over the sounds of our neighbouring diners! We followed Shani's steps as she led us to John Lennon's memorial gardens at Strawberry Fields in Central Park, and then she took us to a live butterfly exhibition, where we watched as the beautifully coloured insects landed on Eva, laughing at her ecstatic reaction. We loved this city, feeling the exciting vibe that pulsed down Broadway, and were sad when our time in New York was up.

On our flight to Heathrow we looked at the photos from the last six months, pleased to have packed so much into half a year of travel. We were now owners of a gorgeous beachside apartment in Panama, and we were thrilled by the thought that our little boy would soon be joining our family.

Chapter 18
No Pressure!

I had a two-day window to give birth to my child, or at least that was the only time Stuart would be free if he wanted to be present for the birth of one of his three children. Upon our return to the UK I had immediately returned to teaching at my favourite school, this time on a two-month contract, with the end date two days after our son's due date. I was happy to be there, with Naomi as my colleague and lunchtime date. Before I knew it, my contract was finished and they were sending me packing, with cards, flowers and baby clothes.

My mum had come over again to help and we both searched the internet, looking for ideas to get the baby moving. My two-day window was upon us and I knew that Daddy desperately wanted to be there for the birth. I watched YouTube clips and consulted baby websites, seeking other women's advice on how to induce our child naturally. I performed some serious bouncing dance moves, as well as receiving acupressure on my feet and legs … and it worked! A few hours later I woke up beside Stuart, knowing that I was in labour. After making sure that Eva was still asleep and looked after by my mum, we were off to the hospital.

As I entered the delivery suite, one of the nurses attempted to redirect me to the new midwifery-led birthing unit. But I was aware that they couldn't administer epidurals there and politely declined their invitation, registering my name at the reception and immediately asking for drug relief – I could already feel the back pain coming on strong. Not wanting a repeat performance of my last birth, I intended to get help as early as possible rather than waiting until it was too late.

After two painful attempts, where the anaesthetic was carefully placed via a curved needle in the matter beside my spinal cord, I finally had my pain-relief, and giving birth to my little boy would be a wonderful experience. Stuart was beside me throughout the birth, then cut the cord to separate mum from child, and he was happy to be present as our son took his first breath. Max was a healthy little baby. After hours of waiting, due to me losing too much blood after the birth, everything stabilised and we were allowed to leave the hospital. We returned to the farm in the early morning hours to introduce Max to his sister and grandmama.

It had been a busy weekend, not only due to Max's arrival, but because the Commonwealth was celebrating the Diamond Jubilee of Queen Elizabeth II. England was revelling in a four-day event to mark the 60th anniversary of the Queen's accession. When we went to register Max's birth a few days later, in order to get the paperwork to start the passport procedures, we were surprised when we were given a chalice wrapped in a blue, silk-lined box ... from the Queen! Max was proclaimed a Diamond Jubilee baby.

After my mum left, Amber came over with her ten-month-old son, Brodie. It was great to have my girlfriend near, even if the living quarters of our mobile home were small and squished for three adults and three children. In the days that followed we drove to Duncan and Wendy's place, getting together there with Adel and Tony and their gorgeous two-year-old boy, Marley. They had just arrived for a break in the UK, having moved the previous year to Tony's country of birth, Australia. We celebrated Stuart's 40th birthday, inviting everyone to our place for a barbecue, and I slowly started to feel myself again, enjoying the high spirits of all our friends. I felt calmer and didn't stress as much with Max as I had with Eva, knowing what to do when baby calamities surfaced and not feeling like my whole world was under a black cloud. It was tough work being a mum of two but I loved it, knowing how blessed we were to have two beautiful, healthy children under our roof.

After Amber left, Kirsten and Marie came over from Germany for a week, and the sisters were happy to be in each other's company while we mums looked after baby Max. Then I returned to Vancouver for a three-week period, loving watching Eva run off with her cousins, so comfortable with these girls even though she saw them only once a year.

On my return to the UK, I started to make plans for our six months off, and we finally settled on Panama for the first three months, followed by Canada, New Zealand and Australia. Two days after we arrived in Panama we had our first guests; Marie and Kirsten had come for a two-week stay. After an eventful holiday, mother and daughter left Panama tanned and relaxed, having soaked up the sun as we all played around the beach-club infinity pool. Then it was my time to settle down and focus – I had work to do.

Stuart and I had started to compile information for a book. We wanted to focus on dog training, since he was constantly being asked for help while doing his Dog and Duck Show, and we knew that he had a style of training that worked, coming from his years of observing and working with these animals. I'd spend hours writing and rewriting the chapters, trying to convey his exact approach, a methodology he had learned from the animals themselves.

Writing was interrupted when we received our next set of guests – Amber, Dave and Brodie joined us for ten days. We were pleased to be able to put them up in their own bedroom with en suite, rather than a pull-out bed in a small mobile home. We enjoyed days by the pool with our kids and ate terrific meals – Amber and I complemented each other well in the kitchen, accompanied by tall glasses of wine. In the last few days of their visit we had a nice surprise – Rick and Lisa, Stuart's long-time friends and original Canadian host parents, came down to see us, bringing their four kids with them. We found a house in our resort for them to rent, and had great fun when they invited us all down for a barbecue, laughing over drinks late into the night.

When Amber and her family left, we joined Rick and his family as they travelled north in their newly rented ten-man van, stopping four hours later in the coastal village of Santa Catalina. We stayed there for three nights, swimming in the newly built pool at the Time Out resort, and then going out for meals, trying to find a restaurant that we could all agree on. A snorkelling tour was arranged, and Stuart and Eva joined Rick and his family, travelling two hours by boat to get out to Coiba Island, where they had the opportunity to snorkel in some incredible sites that were teeming with fish. At three years of age and wearing a mask and snorkel, Eva swam beside her dad, coming within inches of turtles and having a close encounter with a whale shark. When she returned to the boat and was asked if she had seen the whale shark, her response was, 'You mean that big fish?' It was the first time any of the Andersons family had seen a whale shark, even though they had completed a six-month round-the-world adventure the previous year, during which they had spent a lot of time in the water, enjoying snorkelling and diving expeditions in Fiji, Egypt, Thailand, Indonesia and Australia.

Before they left Panama, Lisa passed on a wealth of information about the process of writing a book, since she had herself the year before written and published a book about her family's travels, called *Mom! There's a Lion in the Toilet!*. She agreed to help us as a proofreader and became the person we'd go to if we had specific questions about publishing and eBooks. A perfect source of information.

Once all our visitors had left I refocused on writing, spending several hours every day locked away in one of the bedrooms. Stuart and I would go over and over each page in the evenings, trying to make sure that it flowed and that it was easy to understand, and I was so thankful to enlist the help of an amazing professional proofreader and copy-editor, a lovely lady called Ilsa. She had approached Stuart at one of the shows asking for advice, and Stuart had given her some ideas on how to solve her dog's negative behaviour. Ilsa applied this method when she returned home, and gave Stuart credit when her dog started to change from its bad behaviour, happy that the family could once more live in harmony with their rambunctious canine. She later contacted Stuart, letting him know that she would be pleased to help him in any way she could. We had kept this information locked at the back of our minds, and now asked for her help with our book. She made the book flow from the very start, and she made a great addition to our team.

By the time our Panama stay was up, we had done it. We had finished the first step on the ladder of creating *The Way of the Dog*, and would learn of the many more steps we had to climb as the following months unfolded. We flew to Vancouver the week before Christmas, enjoying Christmas Day up at my parents' place with my sisters, cousins, nieces and nephew, and with my 99-year-old grandmother. Everyone doted over the babies – Max and my nephew Ben were only three months apart and both under the age of one, and we all laughed as we watched them crawl over the carpet, climbing onto the musical table to tap on the various flashing keys.

After spending some time on Bowen Island, we travelled down to Sarah's place for a few days, celebrating New Year with her and her family, and added one more fun-loving family clan to our evening fiesta. We had a disco ball, strobe lights, and great music pumping through their new house, and everyone dressed up with the supplied hats, wigs and crazy glasses, resulting in hilarious photos, while the seven children raced around, chasing one another. We did the New Year countdown at 9.30 pm, putting the exhausted kids to bed soon after, and then we adults stayed up celebrating late into the night.

We left the cold winter weather and short days of Canada, travelling next to the sunny climes of the South Island of New Zealand. It was the time of their summer holidays and, together with Stuart's siblings and their families, we rented a gorgeous log cabin by a lake. We'd go on hikes in the surrounding mountains or head down the path between the trees, setting up camp beside the lake, where we had kayaks and fishing rods to occupy our time. It was a great bonding experience, and we'd sit under the stars late into the night, often joined by the Wise family, who had been long-time family friends, having attending high school with Stuart and his kin.

We bought a car to travel north, first visiting Helen, Clarry and Gina, and then driving to the coastal town of Nelson, where we had a surprise waiting for us. My very good friend Naomi, my co-worker in the school back in England and Max's godmother, had recently moved to this region with her Kiwi husband, Matt, and now they wanted to take us away to a remote 'batch', one that was accessible only by boat. We ladies went to buy the food supplies while the boys organised picking up a motorised dinghy from a close relative of Matt's, and we all met up at the designated boat launch, repacking our bags for our four-night getaway.

Matt ferried us all in two trips across the bay, then we carried our supplies from the beach up to the solo cabin, and were more than pleased with the rustic home that we moved into. One of the external walls was set up on a winch system with weights so that it could slide up and out of view. We then sat there, on comfy sofas and with an uninterrupted view of the surrounding island, watching as boats came in from the open sea into the safe, calm harbour. In the following days Matt came and went, having already lined up work before he knew of our arrival, and it was on one of his returns that he added two more people to our gang. Kim and Scott were typical Kiwi folk, kind and generous, and we had a great time swapping stories or playing bocce, sitting on the deck late into the night, with the men fighting over who was going to man the 'barbie'.

We left the island and headed to Motueka. There we met Matt's parents and then stayed at his brother's home for the next week, going for day trips to the beautiful golden sands of Kaiteriteri Beach and becoming tourists in the region. The highlight came at the end of our trip, when we were asked if we wanted to join Kim and Scott and Scott's parents as they spent the day sailing the famous Abel Tasman National Park. Scott's dad was part-owner of a lovely, 40-foot motorised boat, and we immediately jumped at the chance of spending the day on the water. We had heard about the incredible scenery along the coast, but had never had the opportunity to explore it.

So we all joined Scott's family, setting off in the perfect, calm conditions for our day's adventure. We counted penguins as they swam past our boat, and watched as our vessel was manoeuvred into remote bays. We passed incredible scenery, drinking glasses of wine from our cushioned seats while the wind whipped our hair. We stopped in a gorgeous bay and were shuttled to the sandy beach by the inflatable dinghy that was towed behind the boat. Then we walked on the designated path to a remote resort where we ordered appetisers and drinks as we conversed happily about our perfect day. We then continued our travels to another designated bay, dropped anchor and jumped into the water for a swim, feeling happy as the cold water refreshed our bodies and souls. Twelve hours later we returned to port, said our goodbyes and thank-yous, and then drove five hours south, returning to Christchurch.

I now had plans for a girls' weekend with my two sisters-in-law, Vicki and Louise, while Stuart was teaming up with Craig and Ian. The three fathers would have the six kids for a whole weekend, to do whatever they pleased. We ladies were off to the North Island, taking the plane to New Zealand's capital, Wellington, accompanied by Stu's mum Jan, who was off to visit a friend. We spent the following three days walking the city streets, popping in and out of shops, then stopping at some of the many seaside restaurants. We had a grand time and loved our close connection, making the promise to have a girls' trip every time I returned to New Zealand.

We returned to the South Island, pleased to find that the children and fathers had survived their weekend together. Not long after we boarded our plane for Perth, Australia, where we were met by Stuart's mate, Tony. He drove us to his home, where we received a very warm welcome from Adel and their son, Marley. Eva and Marley quickly became playmates, jumping on the sofas and sharing toys, while Max tried to keep up with them, chasing them from behind. We filled our days there with activities, walking to some of the many outdoor park areas or going to the community swimming pool, where we all enjoyed the respite from the burning sun.

After a week we organised a car rental, picking up Jan for our drive south and dropping her off with her sister and friends in her hometown of Bridgetown. We continued south, heading for Uncle Rob's chilled-out farm. We felt immediately at home and we stayed there for two weeks, making trips down to Greens Pool, with its seaside lagoon and white, powdery beaches, or borrowing one of the quads, racing down the dirt paths to spot the kangaroos hidden in the bush. We listened as Rob entertained us with his poetry and we'd often have guests drop in, joining us for evening drinks and often staying late into the night as great conversation flowed.

We also made time to work on the book – the edited chapters were coming back to us thick and fast, and we needed to make multiple corrections. We had to add in new sections – an introduction, acknowledgements and back blurb – which all had to be carefully worded. We chose the pictures for the centre of the book and found the ideal photo for the cover, sending the artwork to a very clever graphic designer, Helen, who worked her magic and made *The Way of the Dog* come alive. It was an exciting time as we could really see the book coming together, and we hoped that we would be able to make our deadline, wanting to have the books ready for Stuart's first shows in early April.

Our six-month holiday was at its end. We had had a wonderful time, even though it had felt at a much slower pace with children in tow, and we now changed our focus to the months ahead. There were big things on the horizon: the launch of our book, the growth of the business, and I was soon going to be turning 40. Would we meet our deadlines? Would the book be well received? We were ready to jump in and find out.

Chapter 19
So What's It All About?

I had always dreamed and talked about going to places like Africa and Asia when I was young, but never could have believed that I would be able to see and experience those foreign destinations, time and again.

Here I sit in Panama, Central America, and I pinch myself, grateful for the unique and special lifestyle we have. I feel extremely lucky to be able to have six months off a year, travelling to places that I'd previously only dreamt of, and especially now that I get to show this amazing wonderland called Earth to our children.

I have fallen in love with all the different landscapes we've crossed, been amazed at how close we've come to animals that I'd thought I would only ever see in books or on television, and I have learnt so much from the large diversity of cultures we have encountered.

Looking back at what I have experienced so far in my life, I can see how my consciousness moved in waves as I travelled through different places and experiences. My psyche flowed in and out of levels of awareness, dependent on what I was focusing on at the time. I would, for example, remain level-headed and pragmatic when teaching, looking after family or planning trips. Then I could release my mind and feel connected with my inner self while I was experiencing the magic of a music festival or sharing carefree time with friends abroad, or when I witnessed breathtaking landscape or wildlife. I'd go in and out of all the different stages of awareness knowing that, ultimately, life is a process of creation and that we are creating every moment with our thoughts, words and actions, whether we are conscious of this or not.

I'm intrigued when I look back at the road I took to get me to my present, and when I relive all the different experiences from unique settings around the world that pushed my ego and my conscience in so many different directions. I wish I'd kept a diary more often as I travelled. There are so many other stories that have faded in detail with time, but I'm glad at least to have so many photos and videos that document my experiences, bringing back incredible memories.

So what have I learned on my travels? Below are the mantras that I have picked up on my life journey to date, lessons that I believe help me to be strong and contented with my life. I hope that they might be of some help, or at least interest, to anyone reading this book.

◆

Always believe in yourself. Believe you can do it. You are the only one that is in your head and in your body, so stand up for yourself and be confident in who you are. If you don't believe in yourself, how can you expect others to?

◆

Choose to be happy. There will always be positive and negative things that surround you. Choose to focus on the positive ones, and have the intention to be happy with what you have.

◆

◆

Be present. Be aware. Be here in the Now. Be conscious of the thoughts that are travelling through your mind and whether or not you believe them enough to put them into being. Don't dwell on the past or on the future, or you'll miss the only moment that you are living: the Now.

◆

Don't compare yourself with others. There will always be people who have more money, beauty, friends, health, education, or whatever else, so don't try to compete. Recognise that there will always be a massive percentage of the world's population that has a lot less – you are lucky, just where you are. There is always time for growth, so strive to better yourself, not for others, but for yourself.

◆

Above all, be grateful. Be grateful for what you do have and count those blessings daily. The fact that you can see with your own eyes, walk with your own legs and eat food from your own fridge; these are luxuries that not everyone possesses. Be happy with what you have and recognise that 'The less you want, the more you've got.' This is one of Stuart's sayings, one that has always rung true to me.

◆

We are our own creators, fabricating our lives by pulling experiences towards us through our thoughts, words, and actions. We are our own gods, creating everything we see around us, and we have so much power to manifest that which we focus on.

◆

♦

Other people come into your life to teach you lessons, all the time helping to influence your personality as you react to their energy, forcing you to choose your character through your interactions.

♦

I have learned to keep it simple, and when things get out of control, just to concentrate on my breathing. That's it. Just the breath, entering through my mouth, expanding my chest, and I focus on all the feelings associated with this movement. And when I've done this, things seem clearer and calmer and doable.

♦

We take things too seriously and too personally. Once we understand that everyone is just trying to deal with their own existence, we don't have to feel, bad, hurt or betrayed when others react negatively. We need to be patient with ourselves and with others, otherwise we end up stressed and frustrated, and that's no good for anyone.

♦

We are special. It has taken an immeasurable series of events to get us to the point where we are now, consciously creating this world, so treat your body and your soul with respect, filling them both daily with positive, nourishing substance.

♦

Stuart and I are now in a challenging but incredibly rewarding phase. After so many years of carefree travels, during which we were free of commitment and responsibilities, we are now focusing on a new life

So What's it All About?

of family travel adventures. And we're already enjoying a wonderful new perspective, seeing everything through the eyes of our children, while witnessing their pure delight as they take in the beauty of the myriad of cultures, landscapes and animals across the globe.

I never would have dreamt that I could have six months of travel time every year, and I try to remind myself of this every day. Every day I take time to connect with the energy of the universe, and to go over all the things that I am grateful for. I make sure to spend quality time with my husband and children whenever I can, knowing that these moments are precious and that they will fly past in the blink of an eye.

Stuart and I feel happy at what we have accomplished in the past 13 years together, and we fully appreciate the support of our wonderful circle of family and friends. I look forward to what our family will discover together on our future expeditions.

I hope that the tales of my personal adventures inspire you to seek your own dreams in some small way. Live life to the fullest and make sure you take time to fill your days with activities that bring you happiness, love and laughter.

> *Twenty years from now you will be more disappointed by the things that you didn't do than by the ones you did do. So throw off the bowlines. Sail away from the safe harbor. Catch the trade winds in your sails. Explore. Dream. Discover.*
>
> H. Jackson Brown Jr., *P.S. I Love You*

Coming soon . . .

The Adventures of Duke and Dolly

Based on the stars of the Dog and Duck Show, this series of children's books tells the story of a unique friendship between a Border Collie and a duck, and their quest to return home.

Join Duke and Dolly as they travel the globe, discovering new countries and learning about life while they are on their exciting journey.

For more information on the **Dog and Duck Show**, see our website www.doganduckshow.com

Printed in Great Britain
by Amazon